When FOOTBALL *Was* FOOTBALL

WOLVES

First published in 2012

A catalogue record for this book is available from the British Library

ISBN: 978-0-857331-72-4

Published by Haynes Publishing, Sparkford, Yeovil,
Somerset BA22 7JJ, UK
Tel: 01963 442030 Fax: 01963 440001
Int. tel: +44 1963 442030 Int. fax: +44 1963 440001
E-mail: sales@haynes.co.uk
Website: www.haynes.co.uk

Haynes North America Inc., 861 Lawrence Drive,
Newbury Park, California 91320, USA

Images © Mirrorpix

Creative Director: Kevin Gardner
Designed for Haynes by BrainWave

Printed and bound in the US

When FOOTBALL *Was* FOOTBALL

WOLVES

A Nostalgic Look at a Century of the Club

David Instone

Contents

Although I'm from the rugby league town of Warrington, I was a distant supporter of Wolverhampton Wanderers because my best friend's dad was from the town. My early affection for the club was confirmed when one of my first chewing gum cards just happened to feature the Wolves and England captain, Billy Wright. His picture was my prized possession.

A decade on and I arrived at Molineux, with my only knowledge of the late 1960s players courtesy of photographs in football magazines and the occasional viewing on television. A vivid image in my mind was one of Derek Dougan raising his hands to the North Bank after flicking the ball up and volleying it into the net past the Hull goalkeeper.

"Sometimes I wish I could freeze the picture" is a line from one of the songs of the *Mamma Mia* film, and that's something this dramatic history of Wolves certainly achieves.

I know there won't be many around with memories of pre-Second World War games but it is fascinating to see the style of kit, the type of boots, ball and so on – and, indeed, the shape of the players themselves. Defenders were inevitably the big stocky ones while those with the leaner, slimmer physiques were the wingers and inside-forwards.

In my experience, supporters remember more about matches than players do. I've lost count of the number of fans who have started off a conversation with "What about that game in 1973 when you scored against…" And they go on to describe the goal in great detail and the move leading up to it.

So, I can guarantee the 200-plus pictures in this book will do more than underline what expert cameramen, the *Daily Mirror* and its associated titles have done over the decades. They will also undoubtedly bring back some vivid and very special memories for so many.

A lot of the images are new to me and flicking through these pages has been a delight. A certain goal in March 1974 is my obvious favourite but the offbeat snaps are terrific as well. There's one that confirms what George Berry said all those years ago – that I was never going to have a post-playing career as a hair stylist. As for that tender moment captured through the North Bank goal net… well, I didn't even imagine the snappers were tracking the WAGs that long ago!

Footballers get used to seeing photos of themselves in print but I'm sure none of us will tire of seeing these. It's an old cliché that a picture paints a thousand words and this book perfectly captures the illustrious and exciting history of one of the most famous football clubs in the world. Enjoy.

John Richards

Getting that Winning Habit Early
1877-1900

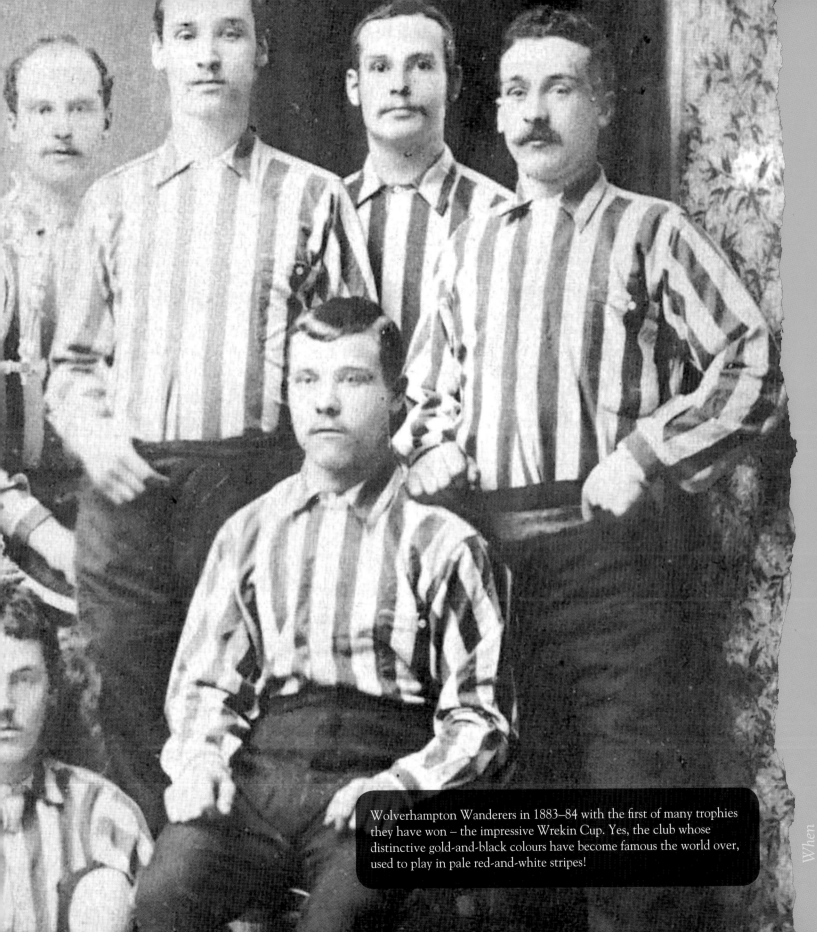

Wolverhampton Wanderers in 1883–84 with the first of many trophies they have won – the impressive Wrekin Cup. Yes, the club whose distinctive gold-and-black colours have become famous the world over, used to play in pale red-and-white stripes!

1877 formation of the club following a meeting of scholars and choristers at St Luke's School in the Blakenhall area of Wolverhampton. 1883 Wolves and Albion meet for the first time (in the Birmingham Senior Cup); Long Eaton Rangers are defeated in Wolves' first FA Cup tie. 1887 Charlie Mason plays for England v Ireland and becomes the Wolves' first international player. 1888 Wolves, one of the 12 founder members of the league, draw 1-1 at home to Aston Villa in their first league game; Wolves beat Albion 2-1 in the first league meeting of the clubs. 1889 Wolves appear in their first FA Cup final, losing 3-0 to Preston at the Oval; Wolves use Molineux for the first time as a permanent home, having previously had several grounds, including Dudley Road. 1893 Wolves are FA Cup finalists again, this time beating Everton 1-0 at Fallowfield, Manchester. 1895 Harry Wood, already a veteran, becomes the first player to reach the 100-goal mark for the Wolves in league and cup games. 1896 The Wolves' third FA Cup final appearance ends in a 2-1 defeat by Sheffield Wednesday at Crystal Palace; Jack Addenbrooke takes charge as team manager, having been club secretary – a role he continued to carry out for more than a decade.

Field of dreams

The land that became some of the most famous acres in English football. This 1871 photograph, taken from near where the Asda superstore now stands, shows the Molineux Hotel, and the pleasure gardens, complete with boating lake, that used to provide recreation of a more gentle kind. In the distance on the left is St Peter's Church.

Wolves have the final say

Not only were the Wolves among the 12 founding clubs when the Football League was formed in 1888, they also emerged as early winners of silverware by lifting the FA Cup, for the first of their four times to date, when they beat Everton by the only goal of the final at Fallowfield, Manchester, five years later. The club had lost the 1889 final to Preston North End and their victorious 1893 players were later honoured by having their names put onto plaques on houses in a road named Wanderers Avenue, which was built on the site of their former ground near the Fighting Cocks in the Blakenhall area of the town.

RIGHT: The match ball from the 1893 FA Cup final – despatched between Everton's posts to decisive effect by the scorer of the only goal, captain Harry Allen.

BELOW: An early item of memorabilia – Wolves' FA Cup heroes are honoured.

FA Cup final 1889

Date & Venue: 30th March 1889 at the Oval.

Result: Wolves (0) 0 Preston North End (2) 3.

Wolves: Baynton, Baugh, Mason, Fletcher, Allen, Lowder, Hunter, Wykes, Brodie, Wood, Knight.

Preston North End: Mills-Roberts, Howarth, Holmes, Drummond, Russell, Graham, Gordon, Ross, Goodall, Thomson, Dewhurst.

Goals: Dewhurst (15 min), Ross (25 min), Thomson (70 min).

Attendance: 22,250.

Captain: Harry Allen.

Manager: Committee.

The boots worn by Wolves winger David Black in the 2-1 FA Cup final defeat against Sheffield Wednesday at Crystal Palace in 1896. Ayrshire-born Black played once for Scotland, used to live in Red Cross Street right next to Molineux and has a grandson, Malcolm, who remains a season ticket holder. Not only did Black apply Dubbin to his match-day footwear but he would also stand in hot water wearing his boots to increase their suppleness.

FA Cup final 1893

Date & Venue: 25th March 1893 at Fallowfield, Manchester.

Result: Everton (0) 0 Wolves (0) 1.

Everton: Williams, Kelso, Howarth, Boyle, Holt, Stewart, Latta, Gordon, Maxwell, Chadwick, Milward.

Wolves: Rose, Baugh, Swift, Malpass, Allen, Kinsey, Topham, Wykes, Butcher, Wood, Griffin.

Goal: Allen (60 min).

Attendance: 45,067.

Captain: Harry Allen.

Manager: Committee.

FA Cup final 1896

Date & Venue: 18th April 1896 at Crystal Palace.

Result: Sheffield Wednesday (2) 2 Wolves (1) 1.

Sheffield Wednesday: Massey, Earp, Langley, Brandon, Crawshaw, Petrie, Brash, Brady, Bell, Davis, Spiksley.

Wolves: Tennant, Baugh, Dunn, Griffiths, Malpass, Owen, Tonks, Henderson, Beats, Wood, Black.

Goals: Spiksley (2 min), Black (10 min), Spiksley (18 min).

Attendance: 48,836.

Captain: Harry Wood.

Manager: Committee.

Stripe-shirted Wolves forwards, at least now properly attired in gold and black, bear down on goal as Crystal Palace survive a near thing. This 1909 tie broke the Wanderers' grip on the FA Cup and came at a time when they had been relegated to Division Two, where the fixture list included the likes of Gainsborough Trinity, Glossop and Clapton Orient.

1906 Wolves finish bottom of Division One and are relegated despite winning 6-1 and 7-0 in their last two games. **1908** Wolves are FA Cup winners again after beating Newcastle 3-1 in the final at Crystal Palace. One of their scorers is an amateur, the Reverend Kenneth Hunt. **1915** The club's last game before the First World War wipes out the league programme for four seasons. **1920** Albert Bishop plays the last of his – then club record – 382 matches for Wolves.

Molineux, Wolverhampton Wanderers' home from 1889, is pictured in 1905. The people from health and safety would have had a field day…

Cup kings

Wolves, having had a fallow decade and a bit in the FA Cup, were back in the spotlight – such as it was – after beating Bradford City, Bury, Swindon Town, Stoke City and Southampton to reach the final of the 1907–08 competition. They were not expected to be able to beat Newcastle United at Crystal Palace but they had a secret weapon, a football-loving clergyman. The Reverend Kenneth Hunt, a renowned schoolmaster, played throughout his career as an amateur and added two full England caps to the 20 he won in the amateur side. The six-footer played 61 games for Wolves, by far the most memorable of which was the 1908 final, in which he scored one of the goals in his club's 3-1 victory. His team-mates weren't too impressed when, upon their return to Wolverhampton, they were taken back to the vicarage at St Mark's Church and had to wait to celebrate their surprise success in the time-honoured way.

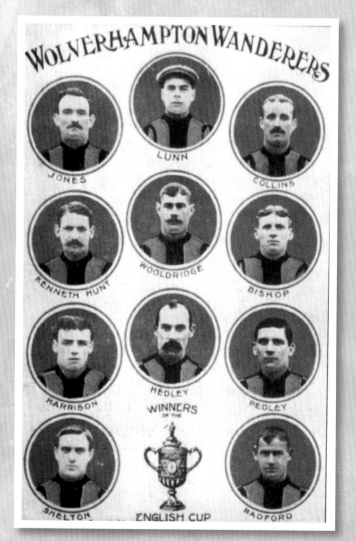

ABOVE: Cup winners again… Wolves' players, most of them drawn from the district of Wolverhampton, are suitably recognized in a keepsake from the time. In front of a sodden near 75,000 crowd, they had certainly lived up to the words of the Revd Hunt, who had promised: "We shall hustle Newcastle off their game."

VOLF "Its a shame to pull this New Castle down – But! it is not the first that has been built in the air." PUBLISHED BY H. PAULTON, WOLVERHAMPTON

'Wolf' pulling down the 'Newcastle' in 1908

FA Cup final 1908

Date & Venue: 25th April 1908 at Crystal Palace.

Result: Wolves (2) 3 Newcastle United (0) 1.

Wolves: Lunn, Jones, Collins, Hunt, Wooldridge, Bishop, Harrison, Shelton, Hedley, Radford, Pedley.

Newcastle United: Lawrence, McCracken, Pudan, Gardner, Veitch, McWilliam, Rutherford, Howie, Appleyard, Speedie, Wilson.

Goals: Hunt (40 min), Hedley (43 min), Howie (73 min), Harrison (85 min).

Attendance: 74,967.

Captain: Billy Wooldridge.

Secretary/Manager: Jack Addenbrooke.

LEFT: A cartoonist depicts the Wolves' unlikely feat of bringing down mighty Newcastle United in the 1908 FA Cup final. The Geordies had a side packed with internationals, had won the league in 1905 and 1907 and would do so again in 1909. Their unfavoured opponents were by this time in Division Two after being relegated in 1906.

The most loyal of servants

Jack Addenbrooke (right) was a key figure in the early decades of Wolverhampton Wanderers. Wolverhampton-born, he was the club's first paid secretary-manager and is said to have been in charge of more than 1,100 matches in various competitions. Almost 860 of those were in the league and FA Cup. However different a manager's duties were in those days, he was at the helm for no fewer than 37 years, helping Wolves lift the FA Cup twice, and make their early name in the game. Sadly, not unlike his counterparts in the 1990s, he later struggled to extricate the club from the second grade and was taken ill in June 1922 and given six months' leave. He died almost immediately, aged 57, during the early weeks of George Jobey's reign as his successor. Addenbrooke's longevity is best summed up by the fact he was presented with a Football League long-service award – and then did another

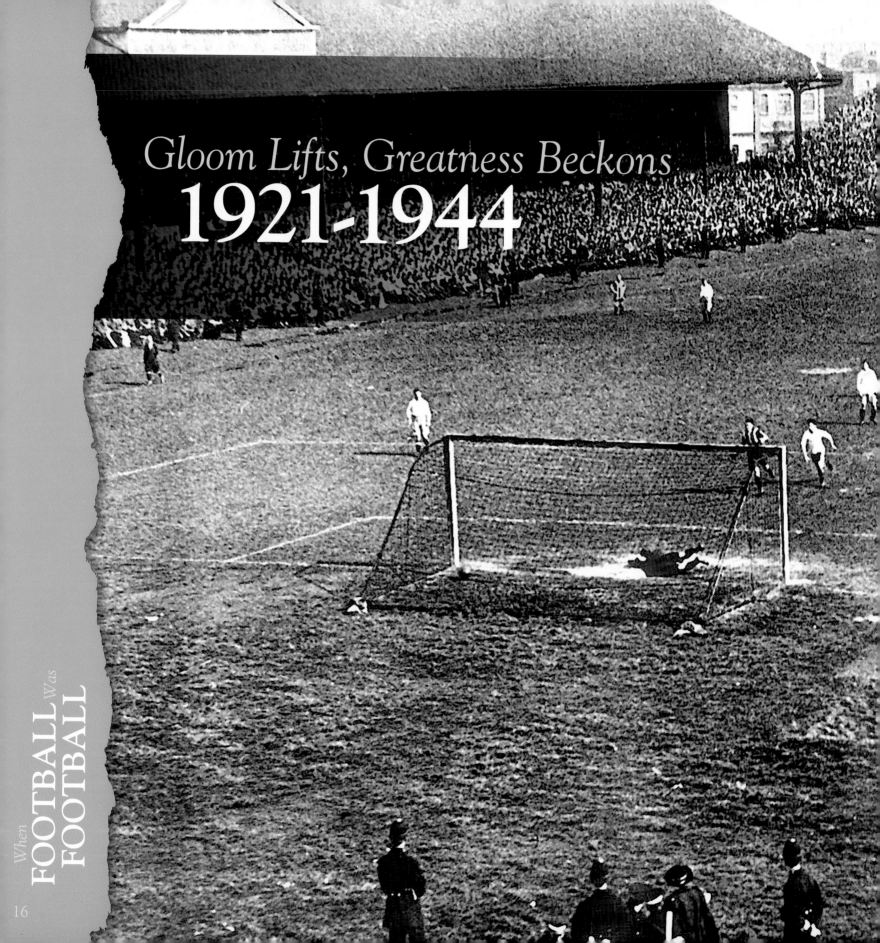

1921-1944

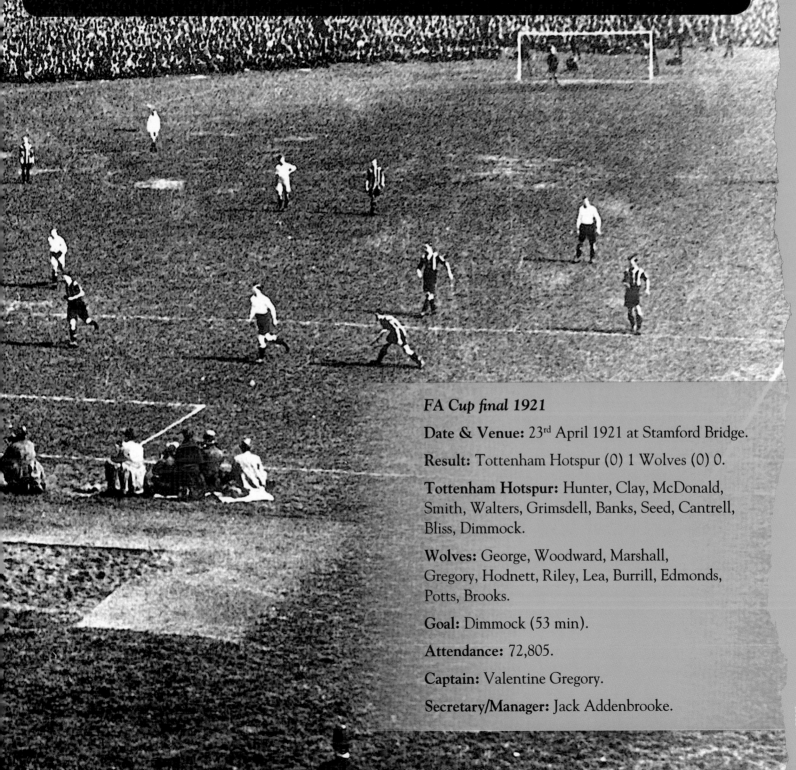

Wolves and Tottenham do battle in the 1921 FA Cup final at a drenched Stamford Bridge. Only two London clubs had previously won the trophy and VIPs turned out in numbers to see whether Division Two underdogs Wolves could prevail. Among the near 73,000 in attendance were King George V, the Prince of Wales and the newly arrived touring Australian cricketers. Brilliant footage of the occasion survives and appears on the DVD of the Wolves' history – alas, the side were defeated by the only goal.

FA Cup final 1921

Date & Venue: 23rd April 1921 at Stamford Bridge.

Result: Tottenham Hotspur (0) 1 Wolves (0) 0.

Tottenham Hotspur: Hunter, Clay, McDonald, Smith, Walters, Grimsdell, Banks, Seed, Cantrell, Bliss, Dimmock.

Wolves: George, Woodward, Marshall, Gregory, Hodnett, Riley, Lea, Burrill, Edmonds, Potts, Brooks.

Goal: Dimmock (53 min).

Attendance: 72,805.

Captain: Valentine Gregory.

Secretary/Manager: Jack Addenbrooke.

When FOOTBALL *was* FOOTBALL

1921 Wolves, still a Division Two club, are beaten 1-0 by Tottenham in the FA Cup final at Chelsea. **1923** In George Jobey's first season as manager, Wolves beat Crystal Palace 1-0 in the last game but are still relegated to the recently formed Division Three North. **1924** Jobey leads Wolves to promotion at the first attempt as Third Division North champions; keeper Noel George finishes with 25 clean sheets in a season – a record that would stand for 64 years. **1927** Tom Phillipson, later to become Wolverhampton's mayor, hits his 100th goal for the club and top-scores for them for the third season running; the formidable Major Frank Buckley is introduced as manager. **1928** Billy "Artillery" Hartill, until 1980 Wolves' all-time top scorer with 170 goals, is signed. **1932** Wolves lose 3-2 at Charlton in signing off as champions of Division Two. **1933** That season's FA Cup winners Everton, Dixie Dean and all, make history by being responsible for numbers being worn on shirts for the first time at Molineux. **1934** Stan Cullis is signed by Wolves from Ellesmere Port Wednesday. **1938** Wolves thrash Leicester 10-1 to record what is still their equal-biggest league victory; Bryn Jones becomes Britain's most expensive player as Wolves sell him to Arsenal for £14,000. **1939** Wolves' first Wembley appearance produces a shock 4-1 FA Cup final defeat against unfavoured Portsmouth; Wolves draw 0-0 with Sunderland and finish second in the table for the second year running; Wolves lose at Blackpool in their last game before the league season is scrapped and almost seven years of competition are lost to the war. **1944** Major Buckley stuns Molineux by quitting and making way for Ted Vizard's arrival.

Feeling like home! That's a bit more like it… a 1920s photo of Molineux showing the ground bearing a greater resemblance to the home that generations of fans grew to know and love.

Goals, goals, goals

Wolverhampton proved a fertile breeding ground for great goalscorers in the 1920s and 1930s. Tom Phillipson netted in 10 consecutive matches (his total tally was 111 goals in 159 Wanderers appearances), Dicky Dorsett rattled in 35 in only 52 outings either side of the war, Billy "Artillery" Hartill had the amazing record of scoring 170 times in only 234 senior games, and then a sort of yesteryear Steve Bull came along in the awesome form of Dennis Westcott, who plundered 124 goals in 144 games. With such heroes at work, no wonder Wolves were a team on the rise. After the ignominy of a one-season slip into Division Three North in the early 1920s, they came bouncing back towards something like their former selves. At first, the recovery was gradual, then they won Division Two as well, in 1931–32, by which time the legendary Major Frank Buckley had taken over. Come the second half of the 1930s and the first fruits of the manager's bold youth policy were harvested, Wolves, having flirted more than once with relegation, were a huge force in the game and finished fifth, second and second in consecutive seasons, with a losing FA Cup final appearance also thrown in. Had it not been for the outbreak of the Second World War, they would surely have become league champions much earlier than they did. Greatness and glory seemed agonisingly close.

Star with a car

Stan Cullis disapproved of his players having cars – certainly sportier ones than he drove – and was quite happy for them to mingle with fans on the bus on the way to games. Almost a decade before Cullis was appointed manager, though, one of his playing colleagues Bryn Jones was happily pictured alongside a handy set of wheels after joining Arsenal in 1938 for what was then a princely world record fee of £14,000. The brilliant inside-forward, as his name might suggest, was a Welsh international. No mean scorer himself with a record of 57 goals from 177 Wolves games, he is also pictured in 1971. He died in 1985.

Record victory

Wolves registered their biggest league win to date when they hammered Leicester at Molineux 10-1 on 15th April 1938. The Good Friday carnage was led by Dennis Westcott and Dicky Dorsett, who each hit four goals, with Ted Maguire and Bryn Jones also on target. It was just as well the attackers were in good form because home keeper Cyril Sidlow was limping from the opening minutes and didn't play again that season. The only time he was beaten, though, was by a Stan Cullis own goal, which fitted into this scoring sequence: 1-0 Westcott (13 min), 2-0 Dorsett (24 min), 3-0 Dorsett (40 min), 4-0 Dorsett (42 min), 5-0 Jones (48 min), 6-0 Westcott (52 min), 7-0 Maguire (61 min), 7-1 Cullis, og (81 min), 8-1 Dorsett (83 min), 9-1 Westcott (85 min), 10-1 Westcott (89 min). Although Major Frank Buckley's side were challenging for the title, the East Midlanders recovered to take a point from them in the return at Filbert Street only three days later. Wolves equalled this margin of victory when they beat Fulham 9-0 at Molineux on 16th September 1959, so avenging a 3-1 defeat at Craven Cottage a week earlier.

Cullis, player and manager supreme

> *You have one life and I gave mine to Wolves.*
>
> Stan Cullis

LEFT: Responsibility came early to Stan Cullis. He captained Wolves at 19, skippered England when he was 22 and became manager at Molineux aged only 32.

BELOW: Stan Cullis' insistence on playing a direct style always caused amusement among the older members of the playing ranks. As manager, he ordered even his goalkeeper and defenders to hit the ball downfield quickly but the likes of Billy Wright, Bert Williams and Johnny Hancocks remembered him as a team-mate who would prefer to play shorter passes out from the back.

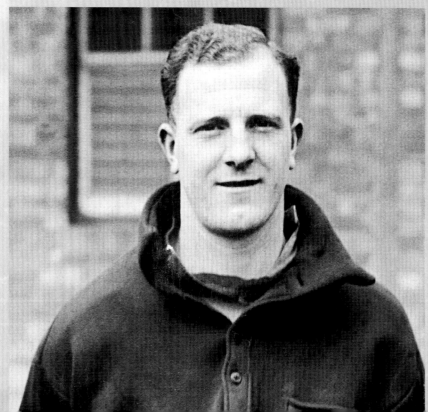

–LEGENDS–

Stan Cullis

Hitler's march across Europe saw to it that Stan Cullis didn't have the fulfilling playing career he had hoped for with Wolves. But the man who was a familiar balding figure in the centre-half shirt before the outbreak of hostilities certainly made up for any personal disappointment with the long occupation of the manager's office that followed.

Cullis, recruited to Molineux as a youngster from the Shropshire town of Ellesmere Port, to which many Wulfrunians had migrated in search of work, was a one-off. He was named Wolves captain in his teens and England captain at 22. Clearly, his leadership qualities were spotted early by both those at the club and by the national selectors.

Wolves' glory years were to come considerably later, after Cullis had been installed as manager at only 32. What isn't so well remembered is that similar heights seemed to be at the collective fingertip for a season or two before the war as well, as Major Frank Buckley's Wanderers twice finished runners-up in the league and were the shock losers against Portsmouth in the 1939 FA Cup final. Maybe Cullis could have had his hands on silverware as a skipper as well…

Cullis squeezed in a short spell as assistant to Ted Vizard before being handed the top job. And, for more than a decade and a half, he did much more than just rule with the proverbial rod of iron. With an oft-stated desire to see the game kept simple, he brilliantly oversaw Molineux's post-war lift-off. First the FA Cup was brought back to Wolverhampton for the first time since 1908.

Then, to the great pain of neighbours West Brom, Wolves became league champions for the first time in their 77-year history. Two more titles and another FA Cup followed over the next six years as the club jousted with Manchester United for the mantle as the nation's top dogs. The conveyor belt of talent appeared endless and Wolves, having been proclaimed champions of the world by their manager after beating Honvéd in the most famous of Molineux's floodlit friendlies, were becoming regulars in organized European competition.

FOOTBALL –STATS–

Stan Cullis

Name: Stan Cullis

Born: Ellesmere Port 1916

Died: 2001

Signed: 1934, as a trainee

Playing career: 1934–1947

Clubs: Wolverhampton Wanderers

Wolves appearances: 171

Wolves goals: 0

England appearances: 12

England wartime appearances: 20

Football League XI appearances: 3

Division One runner-up 1937–38 and 1938–39, FA Cup finalist 1939

Wolves players say their polite hellos to King George VI as they are introduced to him by their captain Stan Cullis before the 1939 FA Cup final. Pictured shaking hands with the monarch is Bill Morris while nearest the camera is Dennis Westcott, the scorer of no fewer than 43 goals that season, including a remarkable 11 in the cup – four in the semi-final against Grimsby in front of Old Trafford's all-time record crowd. Unfancied Portsmouth claimed they knew they were going to win because they saw autographs signed by Wolves' players before kick-off and decided the wobbly handwriting gave away the nervousness in the favourites' dressing room. Whether it was fact or fantasy, Pompey ran out 4-1 winners, with one of their goals coming from former Wolves winger Bert Barlow.

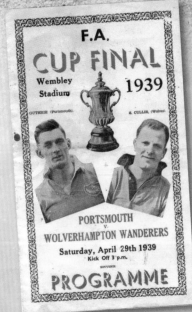

F.A. CUP FINAL

Wembley Stadium 1939

GUTHRIE (Portsmouth)   S. CULLIS. (Wolves)

PORTSMOUTH
V.
WOLVERHAMPTON WANDERERS

Saturday, April 29th 1939
Kick Off 3 p.m.

SOUVENIR

PROGRAMME

FA Cup final 1939

Date & Venue: 29th April 1939 at Wembley.

Result: Portsmouth (2) 4 Wolves (0) 1.

Portsmouth: Walker, Morgan, Rochford, Guthrie, Rowe, Wharton, Worrall, McAlinden, Anderson, Barlow, Parker.

Wolves: Scott, Morris, Taylor, Galley, Cullis, Gardiner, Burton, McIntosh, Westcott, Dorsett, Maguire.

Goals: Barlow (30 min), Anderson (44 min), Barlow (46 min), Dorsett (65 min), Parker (72 min).

Attendance: 99,370.

Captain: Stan Cullis.

Manager: Major Frank Buckley.

"Iron Man" Tells Losing Side "You Can Still Win the Cup," but …

Round Table Conference Plans Wolves' Crash

IT is quiet in the dressing-room as the Wolverhampton players come in.

Outside in the Stadium, the great crowd forget the cold and the rain as they ponder over football's most incredible half-time score.

Lowly Portsmouth, using tactics carefully planned at a players' conference shortly before the match, have gained a two-goal lead in the Cup Final.

Everything had pointed to a smashing victory for the brilliant youngsters from Wolverhampton. They were runners-up for the League championship. Portsmouth had only recently emerged from the relegation zone.

And so, at the interval, eleven players from Wolverhampton sit quietly in their dressing-room, puzzled how best they can fight back against the only team ever to make them look second-rate.

With them is their manager, Major Buckley. The "iron man" of Soccer sees his ambition dashed, his wonder team baffled.

His skill has guided them to Wembley, but now he knows that it is up to the players alone. He can do nothing except watch and hope for a miracle.

And from the man who has the reputation of being blunt and forceful comes no recrimination as he faces his saddened team.

"Well, lads," he says, "you can still win this game."

And the manner in which he speaks makes them go out for the second half confident that they really can find their true form, discover

grand game. We'd have beaten anybody on that form.

"I had a little horseshoe in my pocket and a little bit of white heather down each stocking. I also had a small white elephant mascot tied on my garter under my stocking.

"I said we were going to beat the Wolves by 2—0 and my wife dreamed that the result would be 2—0, but she must have woken up at half-time!"

Barlow, Anderson and Parker have earned the new suits promised by a Portsmouth tailor to the team's goal-scorers. Parker is entitled to nominate another member of the team to receive a suit for his second goal.

When I ask him what he is going to do about it, he replies: "I'm thinking of taking Abe Smith and Bill Bagley along with me to see if anything can be done for them.

"As the two reserves for the Cup-ties they don't get anything, but perhaps in place of the second suit the offer will stand good for them to have some flannel bags."

McAlinden's father and two brothers came over from Ireland to see the game. They just

Apart from the spell early on they showed their real class only once.

That was after Portsmouth's third goal when, realising that they could gain nothing by staying on the defensive, halves and backs moved right up behind the forwards.

For ten minutes it was the old tearaway Wolves, and a goal by Dorsett was fair reward.

But there it ended and once again Portsmouth resumed the role of dictators, playing confidently, almost casually, making that once majestic defence look pathetic.

The stamina of the Southerners was remarkable. If one failed there was always another dropping back to cover him.

It was a triumph of team-work and although all the Portsmouth players deserve praise for their glorious win, I should like to pay special tribute to Barlow, Worrall and McAlinden.

Barlow was the star of the game. He scored the first goal which did so much to ruin the hopes of his old club, and was per-

Helps Club After Mother's Funeral

Knowing that his club needed all the assistance they could get to avoid relegation, Beaumont, Nottingham Forest's outside left, went through a trying ordeal when playing against Plymouth.

Beaumont (on right) travelled to Huddersfield early in the morning to attend the funeral of his mother and returned by road—total journey of 163 miles—to Nottingham.

Despite his tragic loss, Beaumont played a grand game and helped his club to a victory which may save them from the drop to the Third Division.

centre to Anderson was neatly passed on to the inside left and Barlow's shot crashed by Scott.

Even then we thought the Wolves would soon get into their stride. But half a minute before the interval Anderson took advantage of one of the many bad defensive blunders to put his side two up

Head Bowed

WITH his sleeves rolled well up, Cullis came out for the second half yards in front of

The in-depth *Daily Mirror* analysis on the result that shocked the Molineux faithful – Wolverhampton Wanderers 1 Portsmouth 4.

A cup journey that packed 'em in

A whiff of Wembley helped establish Molineux's all-time record attendance a few weeks before the outbreak of the Second World War. A whopping 61,315 were present for the FA Cup fifth-round victory at home to Liverpool, the turnout beating by 48 that for the cup clash with Arsenal the previous winter. The figure was swelled by an estimated 10,000 followers from Merseyside, many of whom travelled south by train. But there wasn't much for the red-and-white hordes to celebrate as all of the home forwards, except winger Ted Maguire, were on target in a 4-1 win. For the first time in their history, Wolves were subsequently drawn at home for a fourth successive time in one season and duly beat Everton in front of 59,545. A colossal 76,962 (still Old Trafford's biggest ever gate) then witnessed the semi-final slaughter of Grimsby to underline that these were indeed boom times for the sport. Wolves surprisingly failed in the final, though, against Portsmouth.

A Post-war Molineux Boom
1945-1953

Billy Wright at Wembley in 1949 in the role to which he became accustomed – collecting silverware on behalf of Wolverhampton Wanderers.

1946 Billy Wright, Bert Williams, Johnny Hancocks and three-goal Jesse Pye make their league debuts for Wolves in a 6-1 rout of Arsenal. **1947** Wolves, needing a point from their last game to win their first League Championship, lose at home to Liverpool and finish third. **1948** Stan Cullis, having had a year as assistant, is named Wolves' manager. **1949** Wolves are Wembley winners for the first time as they defeat Leicester 3-1 in the FA Cup final. **1950** Greatness beckons as Wolves finish as Division One runners-up. **1952** Ron Flowers makes his Wolves debut, thus following the likes of Peter Broadbent and Eddie Stuart into the side; he is followed by Bill Slater. **1953** Molineux's first floodlights are officially switched on for a game against a South African XI; Billy Wright captains England (as usual) as Hungary become the first foreign country to win at Wembley.

There was dancing in the streets of Britain after Germany's surrender in the spring of 1945 and, following the years of scaled-down football competition, which had been seen as a way of lifting national morale

Roy Pritchard, a former Bevan Boy, gives chase to Newcastle legend "Wor" Jackie Milburn in Wolves' league game at Newcastle in October 1948. The side, now under Stan Cullis' management, lost 3-1 but took revenge with a 3-0 victory at Molineux in March, as they built up a head of steam that sustained them through a

Mind your lens!

When a ball is flashing at high speed towards a cameraman, the resulting picture can appear a little cock-eyed. Photographer Bert Abell was getting on with his work at the Manchester United v Wolves FA Cup semi-final at Hillsborough in 1949 when he was forced to take sensible protective action as Stan Pearson's shot was re-routed towards him by Bert Williams. Billy Wright and Bill Shorthouse are in the background, Wright rating this as the very best of his 541 performances for the club, as Wolves were effectively reduced to nine men by injuries to full-backs Larry Kelly and Roy Pritchard.

Once more to

Having seen off Manchester United 1-0 in the replay at Goodison Park, Wolves were favourites and full of confidence for the Wembley final against Leicester City. Hats, ties and, of course, rattles were all part of the match-day garb in post-war England, especially on the day of this major Midlands exodus to the capital.

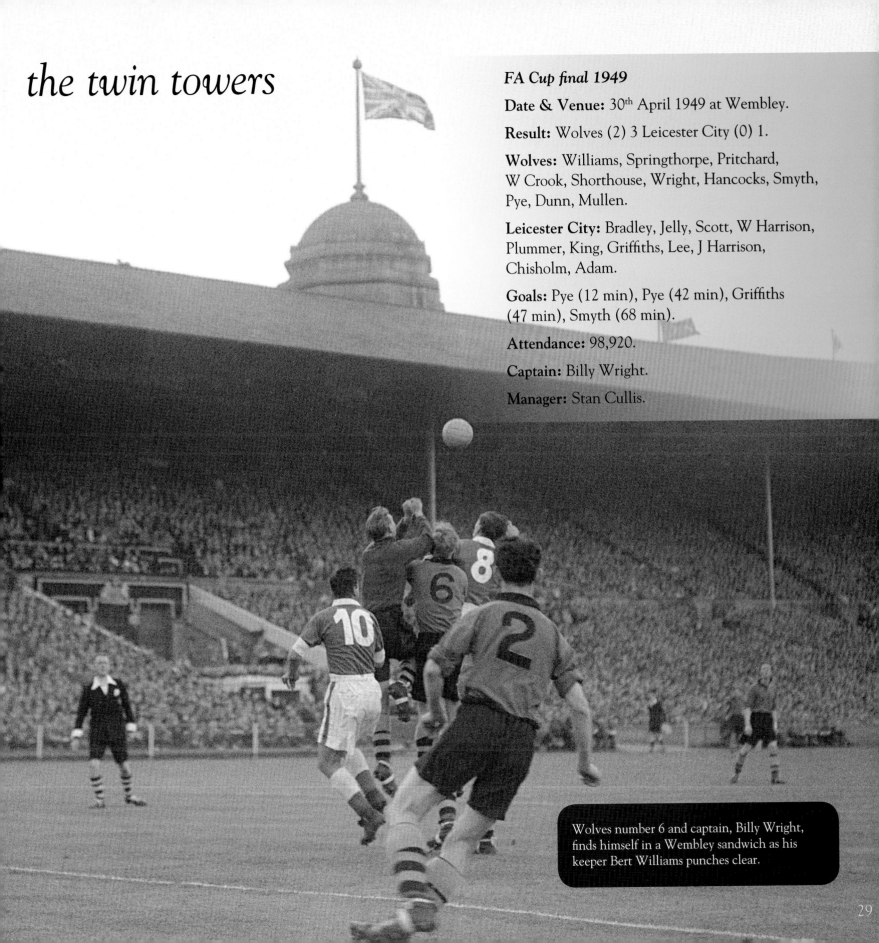

the twin towers

FA Cup final 1949

Date & Venue: 30th April 1949 at Wembley.

Result: Wolves (2) 3 Leicester City (0) 1.

Wolves: Williams, Springthorpe, Pritchard, W Crook, Shorthouse, Wright, Hancocks, Smyth, Pye, Dunn, Mullen.

Leicester City: Bradley, Jelly, Scott, W Harrison, Plummer, King, Griffiths, Lee, J Harrison, Chisholm, Adam.

Goals: Pye (12 min), Pye (42 min), Griffiths (47 min), Smyth (68 min).

Attendance: 98,920.

Captain: Billy Wright.

Manager: Stan Cullis.

Wolves number 6 and captain, Billy Wright, finds himself in a Wembley sandwich as his keeper Bert Williams punches clear.

Magical moments for Wolves fans as Billy Wright is chaired towards the dressing rooms by (left) Bill Shorthouse and the two-goal Jesse Pye, following the 3-1 victory over Leicester, the club the skipper had guested for during the war. The winning of the club's first major honour for 31 years was highlighted by Sammy Smyth, who scored one of Wembley's finest ever goals.

The people of Wolverhampton turned out in their tens of thousands to welcome Stan Cullis' FA Cup winners back to the town. Billy was among those who took a turn at the microphone, having packed the kit for the 1939 final and then been reduced to tears when he heard Wolves had been beaten by Portsmouth.

Keeping the home fires burning

Can you imagine David Beckham or John Terry doing this? Billy Wright shows he is happy to do the chores at the home in the Claregate area of Wolverhampton, where he was accommodated for the best part of two decades by the town's most famous landlady, Mrs Colley.

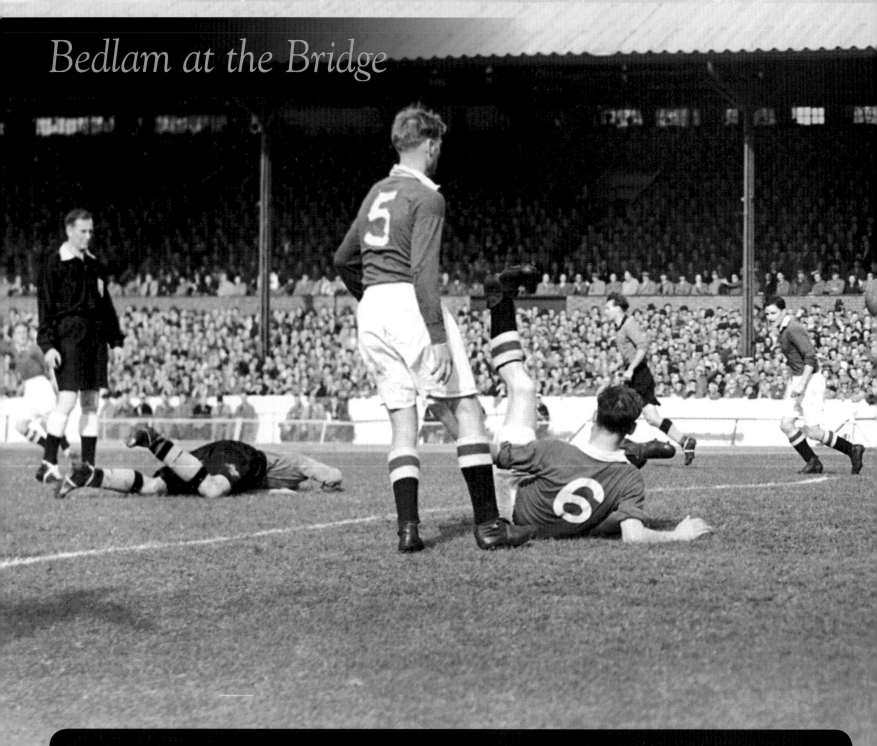

Bedlam at the Bridge

Chaotic scenes in the goalmouth at Stamford Bridge as Chelsea keeper Bill Robertson emerges with the ball while Dennis Wilshaw ends up in the net and Roy Swinbourne also finds himself grounded. This 2-1 away win came early in the 1952–53 season, in which Wolves finished third after two years of backward steps, hinting at the greatness that was to follow.

LEFT: Remarkably, Wolves had at least one player in every England side from 1938 to the summer of 1963 – on some occasions, they had several representatives. For this 1953 game away to Wales, the Molineux trio of skipper Billy Wright, Dennis Wilshaw and Jimmy Mullen are the three on the right of the front row.

In the safest of hands

Ever the perfectionist, Bert Williams keeps his head still and makes sure every part of his body is in the right place – even to deal with this shot in training at Molineux. The keeper was a boyhood Albion fan who first played for Walsall but became a legend at Wolves and received an MBE by way of celebration on his 90th birthday.

FOOTBALL -STATS-

Bert Williams

Name: Bert Williams MBE
Born: Bradley, Bilston 1920
Signed: 1945, from Walsall
Playing career: 1937–1957
Clubs: Walsall, Leicester City, Chelsea, Derby County (the latter three only in wartime), Wolverhampton Wanderers
Wolves appearances: 420
Wolves goals: 0
England appearances: 24
England wartime appearances: 2
Football League XI appearances: 5
League Championship winner 1953–54, League Championship runner-up 1949–50 and 1954–55, FA Cup winner 1949

LEFT: Williams demonstrates his characteristic agility by flying across his goal while wearing England colours at Wembley.

–LEGENDS–

Bert Williams

So worried was the young Bert Williams about growing big enough to fulfil his dreams of being a Football League goalkeeper that he used to hang by his arms from a ceiling in the hope of stretching himself and making up the extra inches.

It was an early sign of the fanaticism of this born athlete – a show of determination from a boy who blossomed into a man full of daring and agility, one admired the world over. Williams made his way in the game at Walsall and was on the brink of joining Chelsea, a club he served in wartime football, until deciding he didn't want to leave his wife behind in the Midlands, even temporarily.

The Londoners' loss was very much Wolves' gain and he switched to Molineux following the end of the hostilities in time to play in the home clash with Arsenal on the day league football resumed at the start of 1946–47. The side managed by Ted Vizard won 6-1, so it wasn't a bad start for Williams, his good friend Johnny Hancocks, Billy Wright and hat-trick hero Jesse Pye.

The game kicked off more than a decade's duty in the Molineux goalkeeper's jersey by Bert, who is from the same small area of Bradley – just outside Bilston – as two more wonderful post-war Wolves figures, defenders Bill Shorthouse and George Showell.

The keeper went on to appear in 420 league and cup games for the club, playing in the side that lifted the FA Cup in 1949 and followed up by at last becoming league champions in 1953–54. By then, Williams had also thrilled international audiences. Despite having to compete with the formidable Frank Swift and Gil Merrick, he won 24 full England caps in addition to his wartime appearances for the country.

He was famously nicknamed "Il Gattone" (The Cat) by visiting journalists for his heroics in England's victory over Italy at Tottenham in 1949, but built a new life, successfully at that, in business following his total retirement from the game in 1957. In 2010, at the age of 90, he was awarded the MBE.

A low point for Billy

Two years after his superhuman effort at the same venue against Manchester United, Billy Wright returned to Hillsborough for another FA Cup semi-final assignment, this time with Newcastle United in March 1951. The skipper is unable to prevent George Robledo getting in a threatening header here but Wolves survived and were left nursing a grievance following the 0-0 draw because of a disallowed Roy Swinbourne goal they believe should have stood. Their sense of injustice grew after they lost by the only goal in the replay at Huddersfield four days later, the Magpies going on to lift the cup at the expense of a Blackpool side containing the amateur Bill Slater.

Hard though it is to believe, Billy Wright was going through a crisis of confidence at the time of this 3-2 defeat at the Hawthorns. Worried about his timing and his tackling, the club and England captain had to wait until Wolves' long tour of South Africa a few weeks later to return to the imperious sort of form for which he is remembered. The side's fortunes suffered as well, this loss despite a Bert Williams punch away from Albion's Ray Barlow being one of no fewer than 13 in their final 17 league games of 1950–51. Bill Shorthouse is the number 5.

How's that for openers?

Wolves and Manchester City had an uncanny knack of being thrown together on the opening day of seasons before and after the war, and it was partly down to the work of Bill Shorthouse, seen here heading clear, that this Maine Road clash in August 1951 finished goalless. The beaten forward is Dennis Westcott, who had been Wolves' top scorer no fewer than six times, including the war seasons, before returning to his native Lancashire in 1948 – initially to Blackburn Rovers and then City.

> *Roy had got everything - good control, speed and he was good in the air. I remember thinking I would hate to play against him.*
>
> Ron Flowers

Roy Swinbourne, supported in attack by Dennis Wilshaw, heads goalwards in Wolves' 3-3 home league draw with Middlesbrough in October 1952. Both players scored in the game, which was followed inside a fortnight by a 7-3 crushing of Manchester City. Stan Cullis' team went on to finish third in the

Three lions, loads of goals

Dennis Wilshaw wasn't only the scourge of the Welsh. Although the Wolves forward scored twice when wearing number 10 on his England debut in this World Cup qualifier at Ninian Park in 1953, the feat was dwarfed by the four he netted at home to Scotland two years later. Only ever a part-timer at Molineux because of his teaching duties, Wilshaw nevertheless won 12 international caps.

–LEGENDS–

Jimmy Mullen

So popular was Geordie Jimmy Mullen that his team-mates set up the club's Former Players Association in the wake of his sad passing in 1987. To a man, they were hugely touched by his death from a heart attack – an event that left them vowing to meet in happier times from then on. No-one had a bad word to say about this formidable left-winger; a man who was part of the Molineux fabric for over two decades.

Mullen was given his debut as a 16-year-old just before the outbreak of the Second World War and had Alan Steen – who was the same tender age – for company on the opposite flank on the day Major Frank Buckley's Wolves bewitched Manchester United 3-1 at Molineux. Even without his wartime appearances for the club (he made a few elsewhere, too), Mullen played 486 Wolves games. Had the hostilities not intervened, he could easily have played 700 or more. Thankfully, he was still in his prime by the time Wolves beat his former (wartime) club Leicester in the 1949 FA Cup final and he featured strongly in the winning of three league titles in the 1950s before time caught up with him.

Blessed with an extraordinary ability to hit long passes from one wing to the other, shoot fiercely and pull back crosses on the run, Mullen is also among the club's top 15 marksmen of all time with his 112 goals.

International fame inevitably went his way. He won 12 England caps and scored against Belgium in Brussels in 1950 after going on for Stan Mortensen as the country's first used substitute. He also represented England Schoolboys and the Football League, and played B internationals, giving the club an astonishing 23 years of loyal service in the process.

The town of Wolverhampton, where he ran a sports shop for many years, was a sadder place for his sudden death at the age of only 64.

FOOTBALL –STATS–

Jimmy Mullen

Name: Jimmy Mullen
Born: Newcastle-upon-Tyne 1923
Died: 1987
Signed: 1937, as a trainee
Playing career: 1937–1959
Clubs: Wolverhampton Wanderers, Leicester City (only in wartime)
Wolves appearances: 486
Wolves goals: 112
England appearances: 12
England wartime appearances: 3
Football League XI appearances: 1
League Championship winner 1953–54, 1957–58 and 1958–59, League Championship runner-up 1938–39, 1949–50 and 1954–55, FA Cup winner 1949

Best Bar NONE!
1954-1961

Ours again! That was actually the local newspaper headline when Wolves won the FA Cup in 1960 but could equally have applied to the time when Billy Wright was presented with successive league titles in the late 1950s. Chairman James Baker decides that the receipt of the trophy is a good time to light up.

1954 Wolves beat Tottenham to lift their first league crown, condemning West Brom to second place; Wolves thrash Spartak Moscow 4-0 in one of the highest-profile of the club's famous floodlit friendlies; Honvéd are defeated by Wolves – another friendly! **1955** Wolves finish as league runners-up to Chelsea, having lost at the Bridge in April to a penalty. **1957** Real Madrid are beaten 3-2 in front of 55,169 in a Molineux friendly. **1958** Wolves beat closest rivals Preston in their last home game of the season to regain the League Championship crown; England field an all-Wolves half-back line of Clamp, Wright, Slater for three of their matches in the World Cup finals in Sweden; Wolves draw with Schalke in the European Cup – their first game in a major European competition. **1959** England's golden boy Billy Wright becomes the first man anywhere to play 100 times for his country and is chaired off after his side's victory over Scotland at Wembley; Wolves thrash Luton 5-0 to become champions again and make it three titles in six years; Billy Wright plays his 541st and final Wolves game, a 3-0 home win over Leicester. **1960** Wolves thrash Chelsea 5-1 at Stamford Bridge to keep alive their title hopes; Stan Cullis' men beat Blackburn 3-0 to lift the FA Cup and go within a point of becoming the first club in the 20th century to do the double. **1961** Wolves lose to Glasgow Rangers in the European Cup Winners' Cup semi-final.

Wolves and Manchester United, the two superpowers of English football in the late 1950s, in combat at Molineux. Peter Broadbent is the number 10 challenging Bill Foulkes, but just look at that packed South Bank!

47

Champions at last

Try COLMORE for your next motor-cycle

Colmore Depot

The pick of the best makes and the latest models always available. Ride away same day on, no guarantors, no enquiries, no delay. Terms, tax and insurance on the spot. Cover against illness and unemployment.

The Motor Cycle Specialists

20-30, HILL STREET, BIRMINGHAM

No. 2,592

Sports Argus

CITY FINAL

BIRMINGHAM, SATURDAY, APRIL 24, 1954   Twopence

WOLVES DO IT—BY FOUR POINTS!

Albion fail at Pompey: Villa again—find Preston tougher

STORY BEHIND the SCORE
From CHARLES HARROLD . . . Fratton Park

ALBION'S CUP IS BRIMMING—WITH BAD LUCK

Portsmouth 3, W.B. Alb. 0

CUP FINAL SOUVENIR

● Remember the famous BLUE ARGUS—when Albion and Blues met at Wembley in 1931? Thousands of readers still treasure their copies, even if they are creased and tattered!

● A special SOUVENIR of the Albion—Preston Cup Final will be published next Saturday, and that many of you will wish to keep as a memento of another great football occasion.

● To ensure there are sufficient copies for everybody, it is essential that you ORDER your Argus from your newsagent . . . See him tonight!

THE BAD LUCK INJURY SPELL THAT HIT WEST BROM-WICH ALBION IN THE F.A. CUP SEMI-FINAL AND HAS SHADOWED AND STRUCK THEM IN EVERY MATCH SINCE THEN, HAS FOLLOWED THE SIDE RIGHT UP TO THE EVE OF THE WEMBLEY FINAL.

Left winger George Lee was hurt at Fratton Park this afternoon and went off the field ten minutes after the start of the second half.

Lee has a suspected pulled thigh muscle and, if the injury is confirmed Albion will have a touch-and-go week trying to get him fit for the final.

THE VERY FACT THAT HE CAME OFF THE FIELD AS SOON AS POSSIBLE TO AVOID AGGRAVATING THE INJURY IS

KEITH TURNS ONE ROUND THE POST

A 'DOUBLE' FOR THE VILLA, BUT IT WAS NOT A QUICK ONE

From CHARLES MATHESON — Villa Park

Aston Villa 1, Preston 0

PRESTON NORTH END gave a much more impressive display this afternoon than did their rival Cup finalists, Albion, on Tuesday.

It was soon made abundantly clear that there was to be no 6—1 frolic for the home side this time.

Villa started with the idea of playing to the Tuesday formula, sweet and low. So many of their good intentions failed to mature because of the sureness of Preston's marking and tackling.

PRESTON LACKED FINISH

Even without Tom Finney and Charlie Wayman, the visiting forward line was clever enough to give the Villa defence quite a teasing. Laddy Jones and Dennis Hatsell, th, two reserves in the van, were the liveliest of the lot up to the interval. True, Hatsell did not have much chance to show that gift of opportunism which brought him a hat-trick at Tottenham during Easter. Nevertheless, this tall ...

Keith Jones saves the Villa goal at the expense of a corner during a Preston attack. Lined up facing him are, left to right, Peter Aldis, Foster (Preston) and Billy Baxter.

Wolves finally made up for their host of near misses when they were crowned league champions in 1953–54 for the first time.

The fact that they overhauled neighbours West Bromwich Albion to get their hands on the big prize made their triumph all the sweeter, the wonderful state of West Midlands football at the time being underlined by the Baggies' FA Cup success in the same season.

On no fewer than four occasions, Wolves had finished as Division One runners-up – in the last two seasons before the Second World War and again in 1949–50. They had also gone into their final match of 1946–47 requiring only a point to be crowned champions. But, on a sweltering, emotional Molineux afternoon on the last day of May, they lost 2-1 to Liverpool, who thus took the title instead.

Wolves finished third that year, behind Stoke, and had another disappointment to bear with captain Stan Cullis announcing his retirement as a player shortly before kick-off. But he was in the manager's chair when the club started to become serial winners a few years later.

Following another runners-up finish in 1954–55 (a near miss that would be repeated in 1959–60), Wolves finished top of the pile in both 1957–58 and 1958–59 to establish themselves as England's top side.

Page Twenty-Four. SUNDAY MERCURY, April 25, 1954

WOLVES CHAMPIONS — OFFICIAL!

Team's spirit won it, says manager Cullis

TYRRELL TAPS IN WINNER

AROUND the GREYHOUND TRACKS

LEE RUSHED BACK TO HAWTHORNS

WOLVERHAMPTON W. 2, TOTTENHAM H. 0

WOLVES' win finally clinched their Division I championship—the first time the title has been won in the history of the club. Crowds gathered on the pitch after the game, and all the players spoke from the directors' box.

Captain Billy Wright said: "It has been a hard struggle. We shall try to do our best for you next season."

Anti-climax

Defence burden for Blues

Danny as marksman

Side panel

1953–54 title-winning record:
P42 W25 D7 L10 F96 A56 Pts 57

Top scorers: Wilshaw (26), Hancocks (24), Swinbourne (24)

Captain: Billy Wright

Manager: Stan Cullis

The man who captained Wolves to their three titles in six seasons… the much-loved Billy Wright.

The brightest of eras...

A major new feature appeared on the Wolverhampton skyline in 1953 – Molineux's first set of floodlight pylons. A friendly against South Africa marked the official switch-on and the lights were then repeatedly used to illuminate the side's endeavours against a series of crack visitors from abroad. Among them were Spartak, with the TV cameras also in attendance to record the spectacular occasion.

Stars at night

How appropriate it is that Wolverhampton's motto is "Out of darkness cometh light." It was the installation of floodlights at Molineux that did so much to spread the club's name across the world. The club were already on the brink of their big breakthrough as a superpower of English football when a facility that was still rare in the sport was added to the town's landscape in 1953.

It was in the second half of that year, after all, that Wolves built the foundations for what was to be their first League Championship triumph – one achieved at the expense of runners-up West Bromwich Albion no less. But Stan Cullis' vision in pitting his players' wits against the best mainland Europe had to offer captured supporters' imaginations enormously, both in the West Midlands and nationally. So much so that the crowd of 44,055 that descended on Molineux for the title-clinching victory over Tottenham Hotspur in April 1954 was dwarfed by the attendances at the big floodlit games. And, by way of reciprocation, Wolves found themselves invited to become frequent fliers by going to face some of the Continent's finest on foreign fields.

With Billy Wright already long established as England's skipper, it's no wonder the club's name was reaching the lips of millions of followers of the game across the world. Just one point, though: Be careful about talking of the games as "friendlies" in the company of those Wolves players who took part in them!

The Birmingham Mail

TUESDAY, DECEMBER 14, 1954

1 O'CLOCK

ROOTES
SMART CARS. EFFICIENT
Special Wholesale
rates.
ROOT!
Hire Department 180-184

TOP-GEAR WOLVES REALLY GREAT

Fight-back Gave Them a Deserved Victory

There was no magic—black or gold—about Wolves' wonderful 3-2 win over Honved, the Hungarian Army team, reputed to be the best combination of club players in Europe, under the Molineux floodlights last night.

No magic—just grim fighting spirit made possible by superior physical fitness (writes "Citizen").

Let there be no mistake about it, behind all Wolves' triumphs—and their illustrious record goes on increasing—lies that basic, cardinal factor, physical fitness. It proved itself an essential quality against Spartak a month ago; it did so again against Honved last night.

Midlands' Pride

The Wolves are a well-disciplined, fighting-fit side—the pride of the Midlands and an example to the rest of the country.

heads of a crowd of players to Kocsis who headed into the net.

Honved's goal had a number of narrow escapes after this. Goalkeeper Farago, agile as a playing kitten received cheers for superb saves. It was, perhaps, the outstanding figure in this half.

Goal No 2 came in the 14th minute when Kocsis sent Machos away. It was a gorgeous through pass which gave the centre-forward a clear run and as Williams came out to narrow the angle the ball flashed past him into the net.

More Farago saves of international class — the crowd almost made him their hero—and, close on the interval, a grand effort by Williams.

Puskas, the Honved inside left, heads for goal during the match against Wolverhampton Wanderers at Molineux. In close attendance are Broadbent and Swinbourne.

Televising of

BELOW: Peter Broadbent (left) and Dennis Wilshaw were out of luck on this occasion but Wolves rattled in four second-half goals to make sure Spartak returned to Moscow with few happy memories of their night out at Molineux. They were overpowered 4-0, Dynamo Moscow lost 3-2 on their visit the following year and, in-between, Cullis' men hit back from two down to beat Honvéd 3-2 in what is their most famous friendly.

A shrinking world

Wolves players are pictured prior to take-off from London Airport for a step into the unknown in the summer of 1955, when a groundbreaking two-game summer tour took them to Moscow. Their initiative in playing the Continent's top clubs at home and away was seen by many as the catalyst for the launch of the European Cup later in the decade. In the foreground on the left is Bob Ferrier, one of the journalists that accompanied them behind the Iron Curtain.

ABOVE: Billy Wright finds himself with a young admirer during a sightseeing visit in the Russian capital. On the field, life wasn't quite as pleasant for the tourists. They were beaten by both Moscow Spartak and Dynamo Moscow, conceding three goals each time.

RIGHT: Revenge over Dynamo for the defeat Wolves had suffered on their travels started to come with this swing of Bill Slater's right leg. The side were unbeaten at Molineux for nearly a year in all competitions and in the special floodlit fixtures, having finished as league runners-up to Chelsea in 1954–55. Meetings with overseas visitors were still a huge attraction, with 55,480 watching this 2-1 home victory.

FOOTBALL
–STATS–

Johnny Hancocks

Name: Johnny Hancocks
Born: Oakengates, Telford 1919

Died: 1994
Signed: 1946, from Walsall
Playing career: 1938–1960
Clubs: Walsall, Wolverhampton Wanderers, Chester City, Crewe Alexandra, Wrexham, Shrewsbury Town (last four in wartime only), Wellington Town (Telford), Cambridge United
Wolves appearances: 378
Wolves goals: 167

England appearances: 3

Football League XI appearances: 2

League Championship winner 1953–54, League Championship runner-up 1949–50 and 1954–55, FA Cup winner 1949

Practice made perfect for Johnny Hancocks.

–LEGENDS–
Johnny Hancocks

When misty-eyed romantics hark back to the days when Wolves ruled the football world, they inevitably talk about the enormous threat the side carried down the wings. Jimmy Mullen's potency on the left is well acknowledged; equally destructive on the opposite flank, though, was Shropshire-born Johnny Hancocks, a man with dynamite in his tiny boots.

At 5ft 4in tall, Hancocks was the smallest player in Stan Cullis' much-feared line-up. But other statistics are far more important. In 378 competitive games for the club, he scored 167 goals – an astonishing haul given that many would see his role as a provider rather than a finisher. The number 7 had a ferocious shot and, considering the weight of the balls during his heyday, it could not have been much fun standing in a defensive wall when your team were visiting Molineux!

Hancocks played only in the top flight while a Wolves player and was an accomplished penalty-taker as well as brilliantly crossing from the byeline in full flight. He was part of the squad who lifted the FA Cup in 1949 and, in 1953–54, brought the League Championship to the club for the first time. He may well have had more honours for his cabinet had the war years not taken a big chunk out of his career.

And there was an unusual explanation as to why his international recognition ended at a mere three caps with England. His fear of flying eventually saw to it that the only games he would play abroad were those he could get to by sea and land, but he posted a reminder of what might have been by scoring twice against Switzerland at Highbury on his debut for his country.

Hancocks, who cut his teeth down the road at Walsall, was probably at his most lethal in the mid-1950s. Having contributed 24 goals to Wolves' first title-winning campaign, he followed up with 28 in league and cups the season after and 18 the year after that, finishing as the club's top scorer on each of those latter two occasions. What he would have been worth today is anyone's guess!

Johnny Hancocks is a model of respect as he is introduced here to the Duke of Gloucester, with forwards Jesse Pye and Jimmy Dunn this side of the tiny winger.

A team without peers

As if Wolverhampton Wanderers hadn't been formidable enough opponents during the 1950s, they found an extra gear or two towards the end of what was a golden decade for them. The 1953–54 champions had also finished as runners-up twice and in third place twice since winning the FA Cup in 1949. Now they were ready to put the likes of Manchester United and Arsenal right in the shade…

Wolves followed up their sixth-spot placing of 1956–57 by romping to the title by five points the following year. They retained their crown 12 months later, this time with six points to spare, and in 1959–60 went as close as they could have to becoming the first club in the 20th century to achieve the league and cup double. Talk about crowd pleasers – they scored more than 100 league goals in all three seasons and would do the same when they finished third in 1960–61. The margin of their second championship win might have been a bit narrower had it not been for the Munich air crash in early February 1958 – a tragedy that still brings former Wolves defender Eddie Stuart to tears. "We had friends on that plane," he recalls. "*Good* friends." Wolves were actually in Blackpool preparing for a table-topping league game at Old Trafford – their superiority over United already established and underlined by a comfortable late September victory against them at Molineux – when they learned of the catastrophe.

The shadow side United had to field for the final two and a half months of the season sportingly formed a guard of honour to welcome Wolves on to their pitch for the season's penultimate fixture and the visitors ran out easy 4-0 winners. It was success virtually all the way for Cullis' team, who lifted the FA Cup by way of variation in 1960 and missed out by only a point on a third successive title, Burnley playing and winning their final match after other fixtures had been completed. In terms of trophies, it was the end of an era – but what an era!

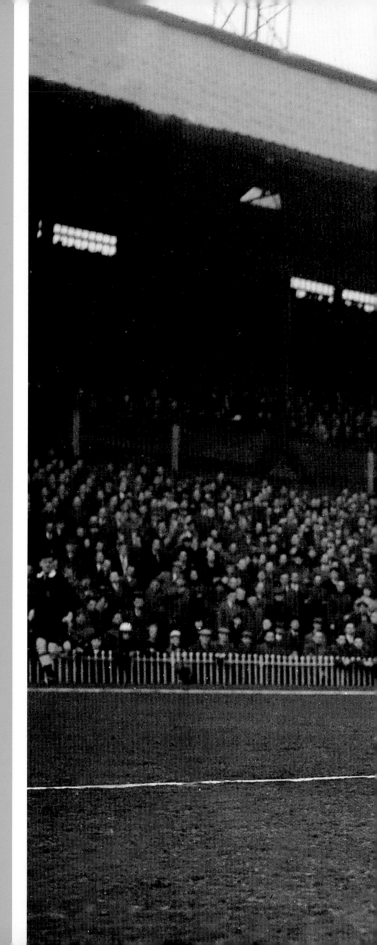

Ron Flowers wrestles possession from Sheffield Wednesday's Albert Quixall at Hillsborough in the final game of Wolves' victorious 1957–58 campaign. The blond Yorkshireman missed out on a place at that summer's World Cup finals but England still had an all-Molineux half-back line in Sweden of Eddie Clamp, Billy Wright and Bill Slater. In the same season, Wolves had won the Central League, Birmingham League, Worcestershire Combination, Worcestershire Combination Cup and even the FA Youth Cup after hitting back from a 5-1 first-leg deficit to beat a Chelsea side containing Jimmy Greaves.

1957–58 title-winning record:
P42 W28 D8 L6 F103 A47 Pts 64

Top scorers: Murray (29), Deeley (23), Broadbent (17)

Captain: Billy Wright

Manager: Stan Cullis

Heading for the
title once more

Jimmy Murray is surrounded by Luton Town defenders as Wolves put the finishing touches to their 1958–59 championship triumph. The brilliant forward, who scored 166 goals in 299 league and cup games for the club, netted one of the five by which the Hatters were humbled.

Leicester City players fittingly mark the entrance of Wolves' heroic side on to the Molineux pitch on 22nd April 1959. It was the evening the club became mathematically assured of their third title in six seasons and had added poignancy, although it wasn't known at the time, as skipper Billy Wright was playing the last of his 541 matches for his beloved Wanderers – he missed the following Saturday's victory at Everton through injury and then decided to retire during pre-season training.

1958–59 title-winning record:
P42 W28 D5 L9 F110 A49 Pts 61

Top scorers: Murray (21),
Broadbent (20), Deeley (17)

Captain: Billy Wright

Manager: Stan Cullis

Billy Wright

Name: Billy Wright CBE
Born: Ironbridge 1924

Died: 1994
Signed: 1938, as a trainee
Playing career: 1938–1959
Clubs: Wolverhampton Wanderers, Leicester City (in wartime only)
Wolves appearances: 541
Wolves goals: 16

England appearances: 105

England wartime appearances: 4

Football League XI appearances: 21

League Championship winner 1953–54, 1957–58 and 1958–59, League Championship runner-up 1949–50, 1954–55, FA Cup winner 1949

So much happened so quickly to Billy Wright towards the end of what has become known as Wolves' glory years. The long-time bachelor finally married Joy Beverley, became a father, and was fêted as the first man in the world to win 100 international caps. This photo shows the player's lovely welcome home from the 1958 World Cup finals.

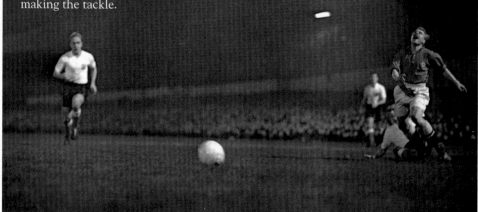

It wasn't only in the special night-time fluorescent gold shirt of Wolverhampton Wanderers that Billy Wright made himself at home under Molineux's inspiring floodlights. He also appeared at the ground for England in this 5-2 World Cup qualifying victory over Denmark in December 1956. Ronnie Clayton is the man making the tackle.

–LEGENDS–

Billy Wright CBE

Hard though it now is to believe, the best and most famous Wolverhampton Wanderer of them all was once turned away broken-hearted from Molineux.

Major Frank Buckley decided that the shy, blond-haired boy from Ironbridge was too small to make it but was thankfully persuaded to change his mind, send an invitation to return forthwith and pave the way for William Ambrose Wright to play the small matter of 541 competitive matches for the club. Wright, having overcome a career-threatening broken ankle during the war, showed promise as an inside-forward before settling into the left-half role he occupied for many years. And such was the respect in which he was held at Wolves that he was made captain in the summer of 1947, following Stan Cullis' retirement.

Billy was already an England international and, after lifting the FA Cup at Wembley in 1949, got his hands on the League Championship five years later. He had overcome a 1951 crisis of form but was destined to take no more backward steps. He won two more League Championships with Wolves and the honours and accolades continued to come his way on foreign fields. He followed up his trip to the 1950 World Cup by going to the finals in 1954 and 1958 as well, subsequently becoming the first man in the world to win 100 caps for his country. Ninety of his 105 caps were gained in the role of captain and the fact he was never booked or sent off is another part of the legend of a wonderful ambassador, whom Sir Jack Hayward described as "England's finest player and gentleman."

Billy, named as Footballer of the Year in 1952, switched to centre-half in the mid-1950s and was awarded a CBE in 1959 for his services to football. Having become a father, he decided to hang his boots up during pre-season training rather than risk any significant tail-off in his magnificent performances. Success eluded him in four years as Arsenal's manager but he kick-started some excellent careers there and was touched to be invited on to Wolves' board for his final years.

Billy chaired off by Ronnie Clayton and Wolverhampton-born Don Howe after his milestone 100th England appearance had brought victory against the Scots in 1959.

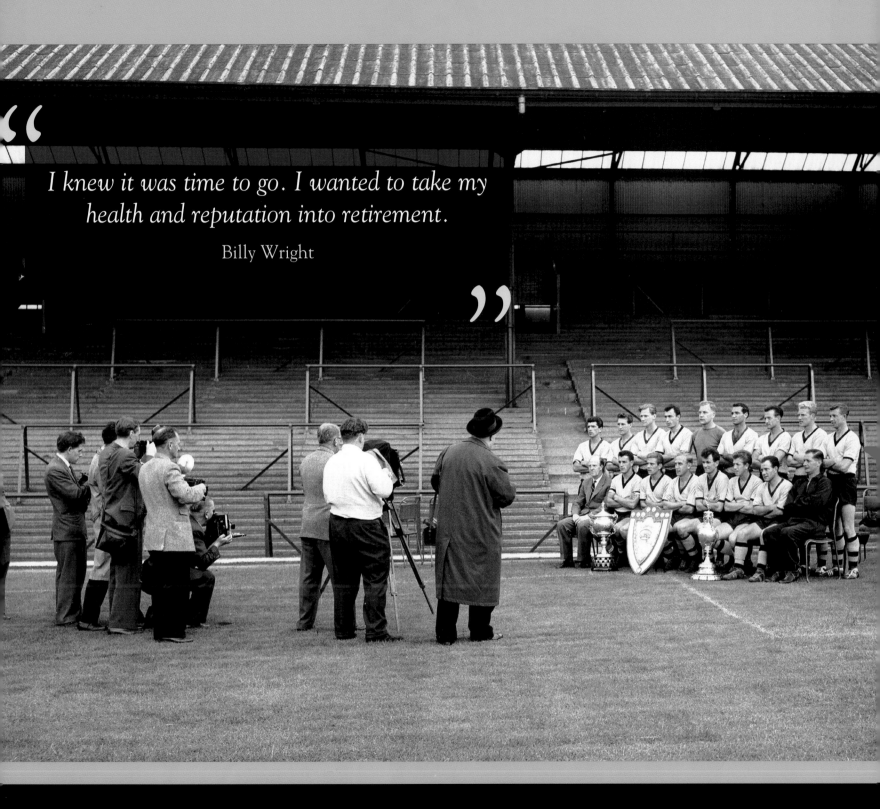

> *I knew it was time to go. I wanted to take my health and reputation into retirement.*
>
> Billy Wright

A picture with a difference, from Wolves' photo call in July 1959; it is not often that the "snappers" are photographed, as well as the players! For the time being, Billy Wright was still there... but his retirement announcement followed soon after.

Manchester United aren't the first English club to have had any feelings of invincibility shattered by Barcelona. In February 1960, Wolves stood tall and proud at the pinnacle of the game, only to find a meeting with the Catalan giants in the second round of the European Cup a step too far. The players climbing the steps of the plane at Elmdon (Birmingham) Airport returned with their tails between their legs after a 4-0 thrashing that was followed by a 5-2 defeat in the return at Molineux. Wolves had beaten Vorwärts and Red Star in the opening two rounds, the club's opening foray in official European competition coming 12 months earlier when they were surprisingly defeated by Schalke 04 at the first stage.

A young Jack Charlton clears on this occasion but rampant Wolves – gunning for glory on two major fronts – won 3-0 in this early April visit to Leeds in 1960, thanks to a hat-trick by Gerry Mannion (left). Jimmy Murray is the other attacker pictured.

Moments of concern for Wolves' stand-in keeper Geoff Sidebottom during the 2-1 FA Cup quarter-final victory at Leicester.

The 48,000-plus crowd at Filbert Street provided another insight into what the well-dressed football fan was wearing – and carrying.

PLAY UP WOLVES

Heading back to Wembley

Bill Slater, by now installed as captain with the dropping of Billy Wright's chosen successor as skipper, Eddie Stuart, heads clear in the all-West Midlands 1960 FA Cup semi-final at the Hawthorns. Aston Villa, destined to lift the Division Two title a few weeks later, were beaten by Norman Deeley's first-half goal, and are represented in this photo by two players who subsequently joined Wolves, Peter McParland (left) and the Scot Bobby Thomson.

Peter Broadbent celebrates as Jimmy Murray, at his side, tucks home Norman Deeley's cross during Wolves' stunning but ultimately unavailing 5-1 victory at Chelsea in the last game of their 1959–60 league programme. Stan Cullis' side were agonisingly close to a third consecutive championship crown, only for Burnley to pip them by subsequently winning at Manchester City in their game in hand.

Wembley revisited

May 1960 has come to be seen as the end of Wolverhampton Wanderers' halcyon years. With their Wembley victory over Blackburn Rovers that spring, they put a fitting finale to a 12-season era of dominance in which they won the FA Cup twice and the League Championship three times.

Jousting with Manchester United for the honour of being recognized as England's top club, they were also First Division runners-up three times and finished third on a further two occasions – the latter placing being repeated in 1960–61. Not a bad record of success considering there was no League Cup to contest in those days and the club's first foray in organized European competition didn't come until the late 1950s.

Stan Cullis' Wolves were also the great entertainers. In four consecutive campaigns starting in 1957–58, they scored well over 100 league goals. It was quite a time to be a regular at Molineux.

RIGHT: Blackburn Rovers and Wolves walk into the sunshine of a cup final afternoon in May 1960, led by managers Dally Duncan and Stan Cullis, and skippers Ronnie Clayton and Bill Slater. This remains Wolves' last appearance in an FA Cup final.

> *It was 85 degrees out there… it was one of the hottest days I remember playing football on.*
>
> Malcolm Finlayson

LEFT: They say Wembley is no place for losers. It's not great for unused squad members either. Gerry Mannion (left), Bobby Mason (centre) and Eddie Stuart have time to kill on cup final day. In those pre-substitute days, Mason was unluckily overlooked for a place in favour of the teenage Barry Stobart, while Stuart believes he lost his regular defensive slot after abuse that was aimed at him and his family following the Sharpeville Massacre in his native South Africa.

BELOW: Blackburn had a young and disaffected Derek Dougan in their Wembley side, the forward having bizarrely submitted a transfer request in the hours leading up to the biggest game of his life. Ron Flowers was in firm control here, though, as he headed clear.

That'll do nicely!

Black Country boy Norman Deeley, a brilliant right-winger who played twice for England, celebrates the first of the two goals he scored in the cup final. On a stifling afternoon, Wolves comfortably won 3-0, also helped by Mike McGrath's own goal.

ABOVE: A rare colour image of the day, with Wolves defending their penalty area against a side reduced to 10 men for half the game because of the broken leg suffered by their left-back Dave Whelan.

TOP LEFT: Eddie Clamp, Peter Broadbent and Barry Stobart breathe a sigh of relief as this Blackburn attack comes to nothing.

LEFT: Stobart and Broadbent in the action again, this time threatening Blackburn keeper Harry Leyland.

Bill Slater, born just up the road from Blackburn in Clitheroe, descends the famous Royal Box steps with the cherished item that Wolves had travelled south for. Behind him are Peter Broadbent and Gerry Harris.

FA Cup final 1960

Date & Venue: 7th May 1960 at Wembley.

Result: Wolves (1) 3 Blackburn Rovers (0) 0.

Wolves: Finlayson, Showell, Harris, Clamp, Slater, Flowers, Deeley, Stobart, Murray, Broadbent, Horne.

Blackburn Rovers: Leyland, Bray, Whelan, Clayton, Woods, McGrath, Bimpson, Dobing, Dougan, Douglas, MacLeod.

Goals: McGrath og (41 min), Deeley (68 min), Deeley (88 min).

Attendance: 98,776.

Captain: Bill Slater.

Manager: Stan Cullis.

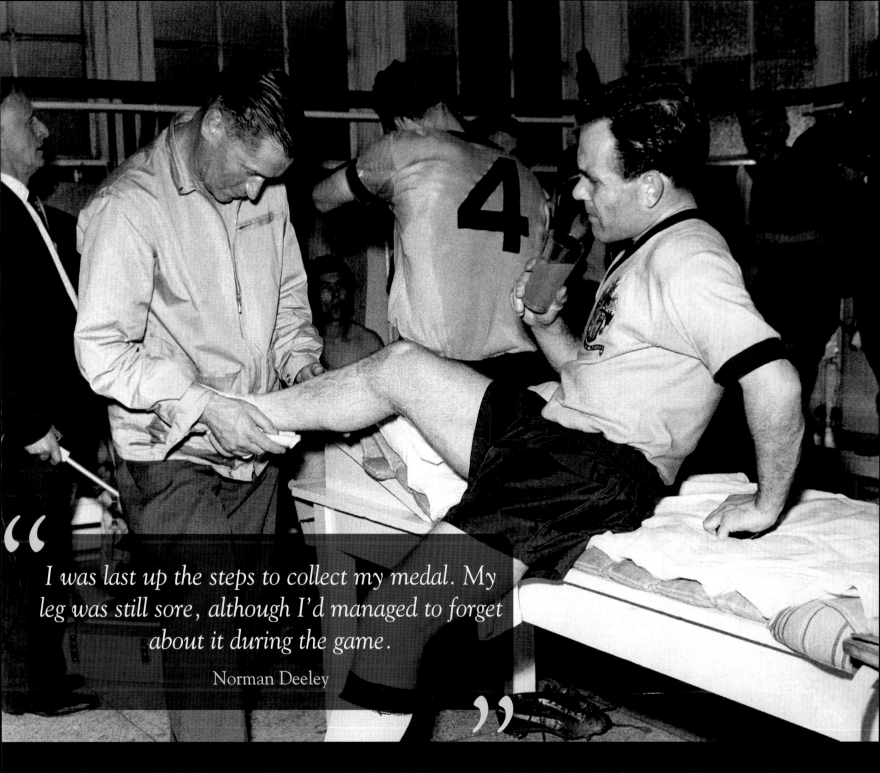

I was last up the steps to collect my medal. My leg was still sore, although I'd managed to forget about it during the game.

Norman Deeley

Relief and a much-needed drink for two-goal hero Norman Deeley as his footwear is eased off in the Wembley dressing room by trainer Joe Gardiner, the Wolves legend who had himself played in an FA Cup final (in 1939) early on in his 50 years' service to the club. Deeley was unlikely to be fazed by playing in front of a full house in football's annual showpiece. In 1959, he had played for England at Rio's Maracanã Stadium before a crowd of about 120,000.

What it all meant

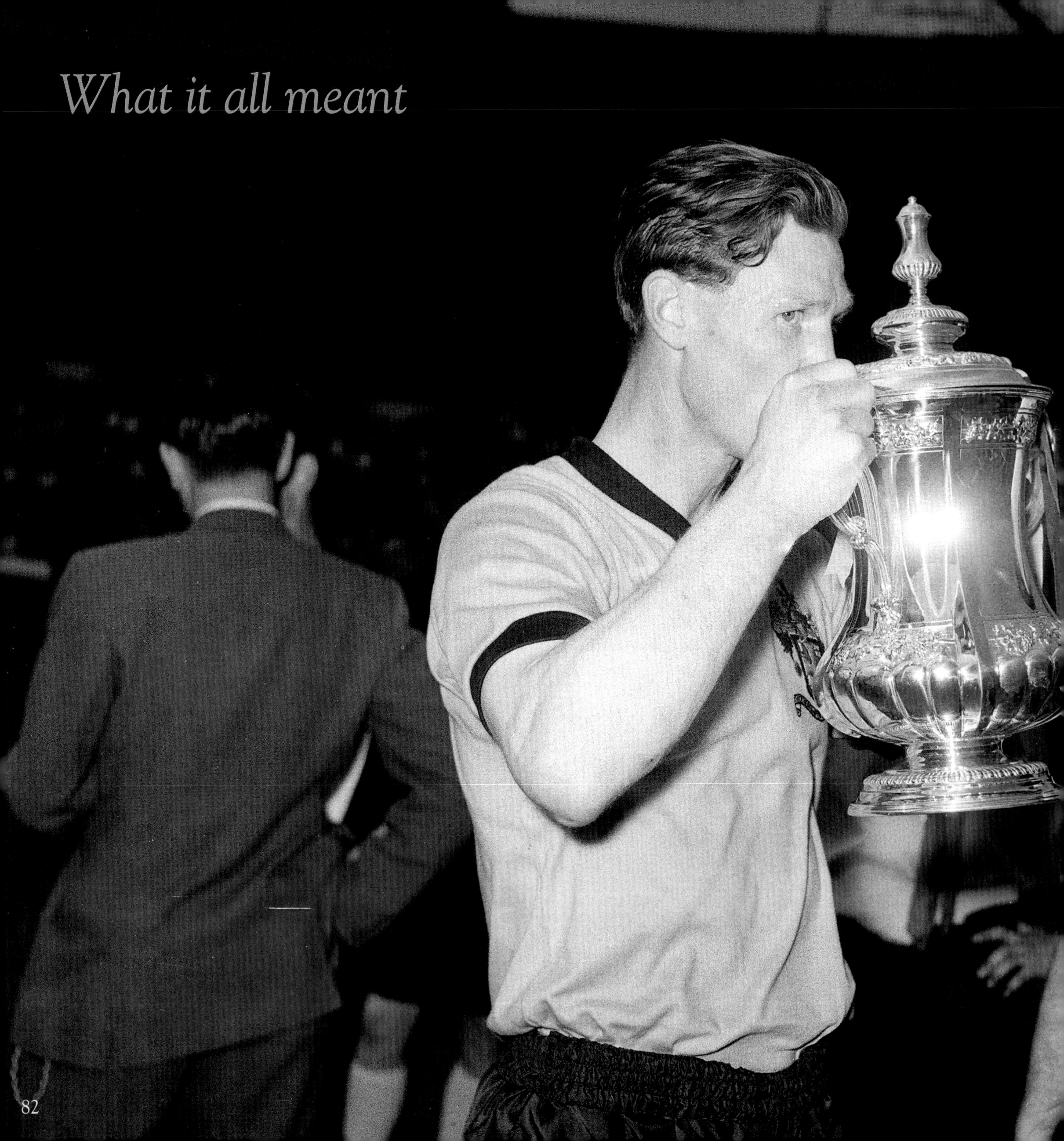

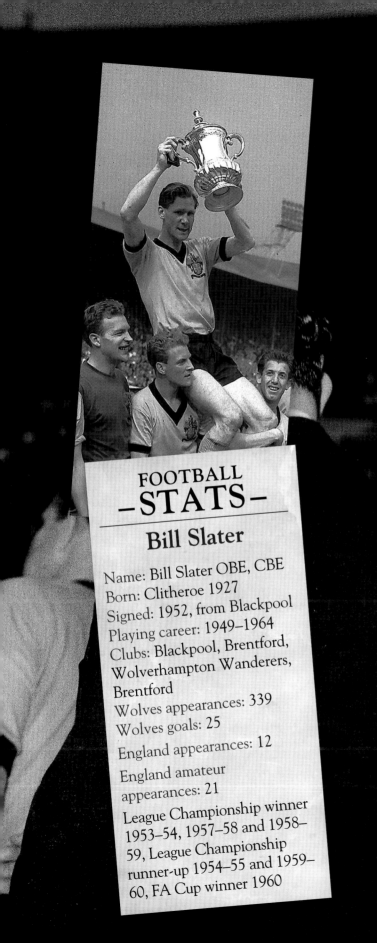

FOOTBALL
–STATS–

Bill Slater

Name: Bill Slater OBE, CBE

Born: Clitheroe 1927

Signed: 1952, from Blackpool

Playing career: 1949–1964

Clubs: Blackpool, Brentford, Wolverhampton Wanderers, Brentford

Wolves appearances: 339

Wolves goals: 25

England appearances: 12

England amateur appearances: 21

League Championship winner 1953–54, 1957–58 and 1958–59, League Championship runner-up 1954–55 and 1959–60, FA Cup winner 1960

–LEGENDS–

Bill Slater OBE, CBE

Where do you start to tell the story of Bill Slater's life and career? With his Footballer of the Year award? With the thrill he felt at receiving the FA Cup as Wolves captain? Or with the fact that he played in a Wembley final as an amateur and was never anything more than a part-time footballer?

It all adds up to a quite extraordinary tale, thankfully a very happy one as he also won three League Championship medals and 12 England caps to place alongside the 21 he received at amateur level.

Slater was born in Clitheroe, Lancashire, but has spent much of his life in London, transferring from Blackpool, for whom he played, unpaid, in a 1951 FA Cup final defeat against Newcastle, to Brentford.

He joined Wolves in August 1952 and emerged as a formidable wing-half alongside Billy Wright and the likes of Eddie Clamp and Ron Flowers. He was later part of an all-Molineux half-back line of Clamp, Wright, Slater at the 1958 World Cup finals in Sweden.

Eventually turning semi-pro in 1954 but continuing his work as a lecturer at Birmingham University, he became part of the backbone of Stan Cullis' much-feared side and was to amass a total of 339 league and cup appearances for the club despite the problems he had in being released for some night matches and many overseas trips. Eddie Stuart was chosen in 1959 to succeed the retired Wright as captain but, after the South African defender lost his place in the line-up, it was Slater who settled into the role instead, up to and after Wolves' Wembley win over Blackburn the following spring.

Slater pipped Burnley's Jimmy McIlroy to the cherished accolade of being named Footballer of the Year in 1960 – the year in which he also qualified as a Bachelor of Science. He had by then been converted to a centre-half and was no one-trick pony. He went on to have a brilliant long career in sports administration. Even that isn't quite all… he has also received the OBE and CBE for his services to sport.

Ted Farmer, already with a prodigious scoring record behind him in youth and reserve football, made a sensational senior debut for Wolves when he netted twice in this 3-1 Division One win at Manchester United in September 1960. The centre-forward would finish his first season with 28 goals, only to then suffer cruel injury problems that seriously shortened his career.

Number 10, Peter Broadbent, scored Wolves' goal in the home second leg of their European Cup Winners' Cup semi-final against Rangers in April 1961. It wasn't enough to spell salvation, though, as the 1-1 draw saw the Scots through 3-1 on aggregate on a night which brought a first glimpse of hooliganism at Molineux for many. The crowd at Ibrox had been a cool 79,000.

Broadbent challenges Peter Bonetti at Chelsea.

FOOTBALL —STATS—

Peter Broadbent

Name: Peter Broadbent
Born: Elvington, Kent 1933
Signed: 1951
Playing career: 1950–1970
Clubs: Brentford, Wolverhampton Wanderers, Shrewsbury Town, Aston Villa, Stockport County
Wolves appearances: 497
Wolves goals: 145

England appearances: 7

Football League XI appearances: 2

League Championship winner 1953–54, 1957–58 and 1958–59, League Championship runner-up 1954–55 and 1959–60, FA Cup winner 1960

–LEGENDS–

Peter Broadbent

To many Wolves fans of a certain vintage, Peter Broadbent was THE star turn in a team of serial winners in the 1950s and early 1960s. Here was an enormously gifted inside-forward who was both a crowd pleaser and possessed the statistical record that backs up claims that he had a touch of genius.

Honours came thick and fast for him in the form of three league titles and an FA Cup triumph, with England recognition along the way. All told, he spent 14 years at Molineux and most of them were as golden as the colour of the club's famous shirts. Wolves' manager Stan Cullis was grateful that the Kent-born Broadbent was recommended to him by the man who had discovered him, George Poyser (later to manage Manchester City). The player turned 18 on a long club tour to South Africa in the summer of 1951 and certainly gave wonderful value for money on the £10,000 he cost.

Having unfortunately started his Wanderers career with a lengthy run of defeats, the former Brentford man took the number 8 jersey of Jimmy Dunn and contributed 12 goals in the 1953–54 campaign in which Wolves lifted the League Championship for the first time.

That was the first of his 11 successive seasons as a regular in the club's line-up, and he had goal totals in double figures in seven of those. Add all the assists and the thrilling part he played in the floodlit friendlies, which made Molineux famous the world over, and it's clear to see that this was a mighty contribution.

Wolves' successive titles at the end of the 1950s, followed by their winning of the FA Cup in 1959–60, obviously did Broadbent's international claims no harm and his haul of seven caps included service at the 1958 World Cup in Sweden. There were also call-ups for the under-23s, England B and the long-defunct Football League XI. Broadbent was the club's first goalscorer in official European competition and also netted in the Charity Shield, having played a key role in the FA Cup final success over Blackburn. His final Wolves game was midway through their sad 1964–65 relegation season.

RIGHT: Broadbent in England training with Bobby Charlton and Johnny Haynes.

Liverpudlian Fred Davies was the man who took over in goal from Malcolm Finlayson and was watched by Gerry Harris as he made this acrobatic save from Sheffield United's Billy Hodgson in September 1962. But, despite the 2-1 victory at Bramall Lane, Wolves were no longer challenging for the big prizes.

1962 Chelsea 4 Wolves 5 in Division One. 1963 Wolves' biggest ever win over West Brom sees them triumph 7-0 in a rearranged game at Molineux. 1964 Stan Cullis, not long back at work after illness, is dismissed in the aftermath of Wolves' 4-3 win over West Ham at Molineux. 1965 Wolves crash 7-4 at Tottenham during Andy Beattie's short spell as manager; already relegated Wolves lose at home to Liverpool in their final game of the season; Peter Knowles scores a hat-trick in Wolves' 4-0 home win over Derby. 1966 A wing-half called Mike Bailey catches Wolves' eye when playing for Charlton against them in a draw at the Valley; Wolves are beaten 4-2 at home by Manchester United in the FA Cup fifth round; Davie Burnside, named in the Crystal Palace team in the programme, scores AGAINST them instead in the first few minutes, after signing for Wolves. 1967 Derek Dougan makes his Wolves debut in a 1-0 win at Plymouth; Wolves lose 3-1 in front of 51,500 in what turns out to be the Division Two title decider at Coventry; Wolves win 2-1 at Fulham in their first game back in the top flight; Wolves draw 3-3 with Albion in front of 52,500 in their (highly controversial) first home game back in the top division; Wolves lose 4-0 and 3-2 against Manchester United in the space of four days in front of a combined 116,000-plus crowd. 1968 Bill McGarry's first match in charge, succeeding Ronnie Allen, sees Wolves lose 2-0 at Manchester United. 1969 Peter Knowles plays his last match (Wolves 3 Nottingham Forest 3) before quitting to concentrate on life as a Jehovah's Witness; Derek Dougan is sent off against Everton and subsequently banned for eight weeks.

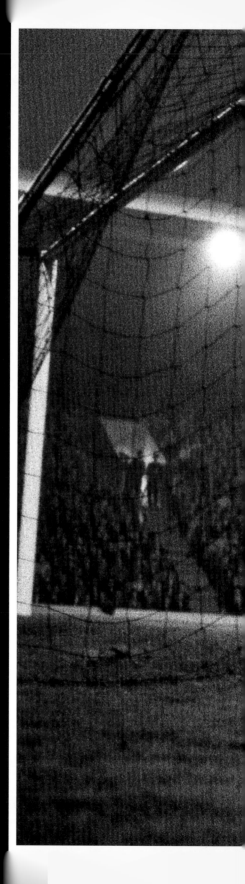

Remarkably, the last two of Malcolm Finlayson's 203 league and cup appearances for Wolves came in heavy defeats at Liverpool. His only game of 1962–63 was a 4-1 loss at Anfield. Here he is pictured in a 6-0 thrashing at the same venue the following September. The Scot actually let in only four of the goals as he had gone off to a tremendous ovation 20 minutes from time because of a hand injury, Jimmy Murray taking his place between the posts.

Football wasn't the only entertainment attraction in Wolverhampton in the early 1960s. This largely female turnout was to welcome The Beatles to the town's Gaumont nightspot in 1963.

End of an era

BELOW: Wolves were a side on the wane when they played this Division One home game against West Ham on 14th September 1964. They had finished 18th, fifth and 16th in the previous three seasons, and a nightmare start to 1964–65 had included a 5-0 hiding at Upton Park. Fred Davies and number 2 Bobby Thomson failed to prevent this goal in the return and, although Wolves recovered to win 4-3, Stan Cullis paid for the failure with his job within 36 hours. He had been at Molineux for well over a quarter of a century.

RIGHT: The inevitable media backlash.

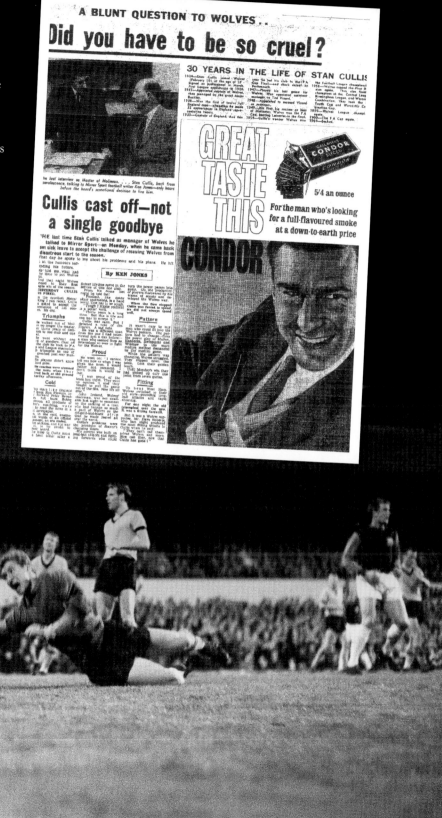

Eddie Stuart, a veteran of 322 games for Wolves and a man who nearly died after picking up a tropical disease on a summer trip home to South Africa, is pictured after moving to Stoke City in 1962. Other popular stalwarts who departed in the early 1960s included Norman Deeley, Bill Slater and Eddie Clamp.

Wolves, in an all white change strip, on the attack in the form of (from left) Bobby Thomson, Dave Woodfield and Dave Wagstaffe in their Division Two victory at Leyton Orient in October 1965. The game was the third of the four successive 3-0 wins with which the Allen era dawned.

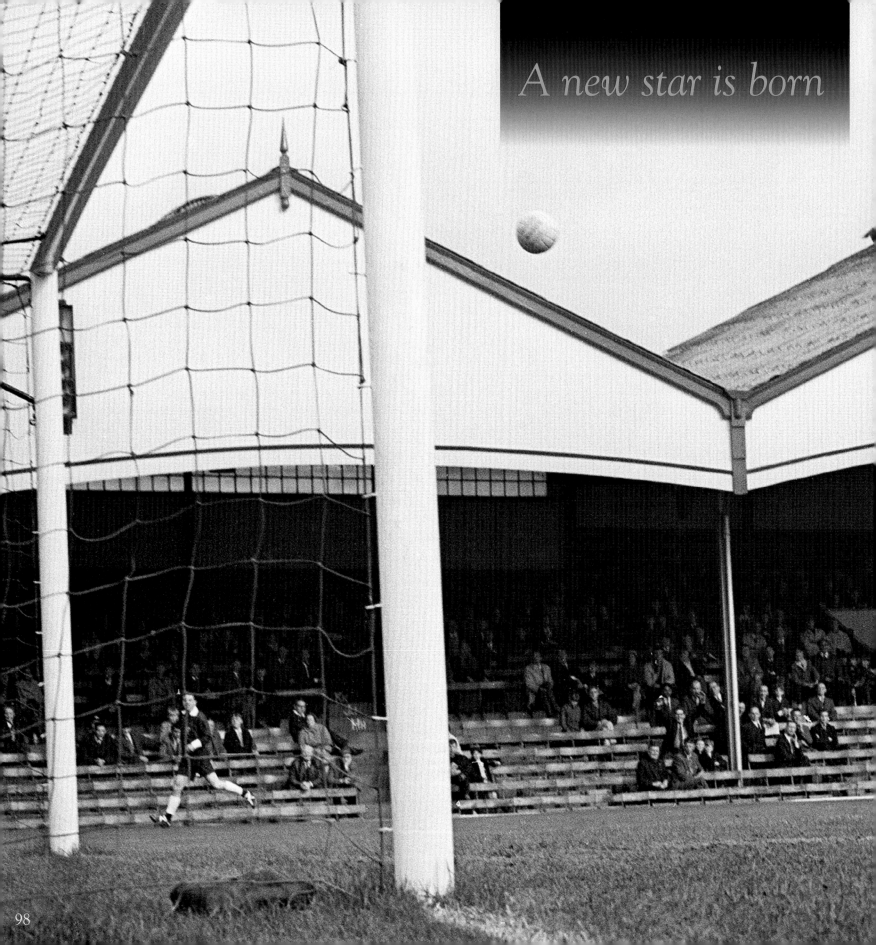

A new star is born

98

Wolves' fans were in need of new heroes after the end of the club's glory years and found one in Peter Knowles. The inside-forward with The Beatles' look, is captured here against Derby County, on his way to his second hat-trick in a fortnight, the other having come at home to Carlisle United. On the right is winger Terry Wharton. Note that the club had by now dispensed with black shorts and switched to gold ones.

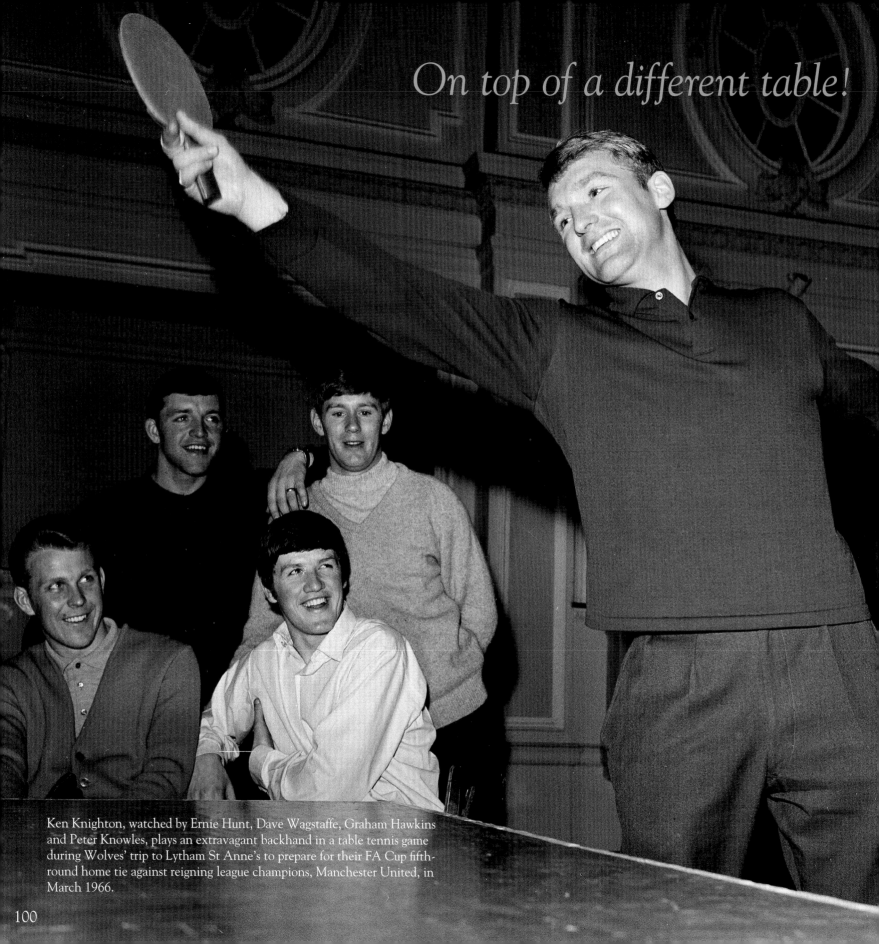

Ken Knighton, watched by Ernie Hunt, Dave Wagstaffe, Graham Hawkins and Peter Knowles, plays an extravagant backhand in a table tennis game during Wolves' trip to Lytham St Anne's to prepare for their FA Cup fifth-round home tie against reigning league champions, Manchester United, in March 1966.

It must have been the coastal air… Knowles and Knighton let their hair down on an afternoon off by the seaside. "Waggy" appears to have no intention of becoming "Wiggy".

The Division Two underdogs drew first blood against United in front of a 53,428 crowd with this penalty from the trusty Terry Wharton. The winger later scored again but the Reds hit back with four goals of their own to repeat the from-behind victory they had pulled off at Molineux in the quarter-final the previous season.

Ronnie Allen was more than a brilliant spotter of players. The man who built half a side for his successor Bill McGarry to prosper with was also an innovator, as shown by the habit of playing cricket to relax his players in the dressing room before kick-off. The manager was the bowler here, with Hugh McIlmoyle the batsman and Bobby Thomson leading the appeal.

Flowers in-between Jimmy Armfield and Bobby Moore at Sheffield's Royal Victoria Hotel in 1962 in preparation for a match against France. On the left is Ray Charnley.

-LEGENDS-

Ron Flowers

What would Wolverhampton Wanderers have been without Wath Wanderers? For a couple of decades, the nursery club set up in South Yorkshire by the former Molineux winger Mark Crook discovered and honed teenage talents that would greatly benefit Stan Cullis and his successors.

Roy Swinbourne, Peter Knowles, Gerry Taylor, Bob Hatton, Ken Knighton, John Galley, Steve Daley and others were all products of this fertile breeding ground but none flowered, if you'll pardon the expression, more spectacularly than Ron Flowers, the blond wing-half who grew up loving his local club Doncaster Rovers, and then travelled the world with Wolves and England.

Flowers moved to Molineux in the early 1950s when greatness was at the club's fingertips, and was a formidable part of the all-conquering side who won League Championships in 1954, 1958 and 1959 (the first top-flight titles in the club's history). Add all those famous floodlit nights, the commanding role he played in the 1960 FA Cup final triumph and his spell as skipper as Wolves went to Division Two and back in the mid-1960s, and he is fully deserving of his place in the top five of the club's all-time record appearance makers.

He is also comfortably Wolves' second most capped England international, with a total of 49 games for his country, which leaves him 25 ahead of his nearest challenger from below, Bert Williams. Flowers missed out on a place at the 1958 World Cup finals in Sweden because his club already provided the half-back line of Bill Slater, Billy Wright and Eddie Clamp, but was in his prime come the showpiece in Chile four years later and came closer than a lot realize to playing in England's 1966 final victory over West Germany. He was put on alert by Alf Ramsey on the Friday night and told that he would be playing if Jack Charlton didn't recover from a heavy cold – which, of course, he did.

Flowers nevertheless scored 10 goals for his country, including six from the penalty spot, so he would have been priceless in today's game in those tense shoot-outs.

Wolves had finished sixth in Division Two in the summer of England's World Cup success and were not destined to hang around much longer away from the domestic elite.

Promotion came under the management of former England forward Ronnie Allen in 1966–67 and the climb back was an intoxicating journey, packed with thrilling afternoons and nights. Allen's side scored over 10 more goals than any other side in the division and fired blanks in only four of their 42 league games, three of those coming in a four-match spell around the turn of the year.

Molineux was once more a great place to be as Mike Bailey emerged as captain as Ron Flowers' long-term successor at wing-half and the likes of Peter Knowles, Dave Wagstaffe, Ernie Hunt and Derek Dougan also thrilled Wanderers' fans. The big time was again at the club's fingertips.

LEFT: Defeats in their opening two games of 1966–67, including this one at home to Birmingham City, was no major problem for Wolves. They were soon flying high at the right end of the table, intent as they were on regaining their top-flight status. Hugh McIlmoyle, pictured here, helped get them going with 14 goals in little over half a season, including one against the Blues.

Striker search led Wolves to the Doog

Ray Crawford, Bobby Woodruff, Hugh McIlmoyle, Bob Hatton and Ernie Hunt all had good goalscoring records when drafted into Wolves' side in the 1960s. None lasted long, though, before being moved on.

It was as if the club thought there was always someone better just round the corner – and ultimately there was.

Hunt actually led the club's goal charts in their 1966–67 promotion-winning campaign and at least had some time to appreciate the charismatic presence at Molineux of Derek Dougan, the Doog.

Ronnie Allen had already recruited Mike Bailey and would later bring in Frank Munro, Derek Parkin and Kenny Hibbitt on bargain prices. But no signing proved more popular in the fans' eyes than that of the Doog, who was their darling from the moment he hit a hat-trick against Hull City on his home debut.

The revolving door for strikers was needed no more.

RIGHT: The Doog watches Bobby Charlton and Matt Busby engage in some street football with schoolboys before the trio attended a press conference in Fleet Street.

Derek Dougan defends himself from a fan who ran on to the pitch and attacked him after he had earned Wolves a point in a 1-1 early April draw at Millwall. It was the fourth of the nine crucial goals the centre-forward scored in only 11 games following his arrival at Molineux in March 1967. Other Wolves players visible are (from left) John Holsgrove, Mike Bailey, Bobby Thomson, Dave Burnside and Dave Wagstaffe.

acceptable in *pitch invasions*

The scenes are purely joyous as Coventry City's Highfield Road home is overrun by supporters celebrating their victory over Wolves in what was dubbed the Midlands Match of the Century. The two teams went up together a few weeks later but this 3-1 Sky Blues victory a fortnight before the end of the season tipped the scales towards them and they emerged as champions.

Back in the big time

ABOVE: If Wolverhampton Wanderers were feeling the effects of a long, tiring summer spent winning the United Soccer Association Championship as Los Angeles Wolves, it didn't show when they hit the ground running back in the big time. They came out of the blocks with an opening-day win at Fulham that featured a Derek Dougan goal, celebrated here by Dave Burnside (centre) and creator Dave Wagstaffe.

RIGHT: Skipper Mike Bailey, who struck a tremendous volley for the killer second goal, challenges Johnny Haynes on a day when Wolves took full revenge for a 5-0 League Cup mauling at Craven Cottage the previous season.

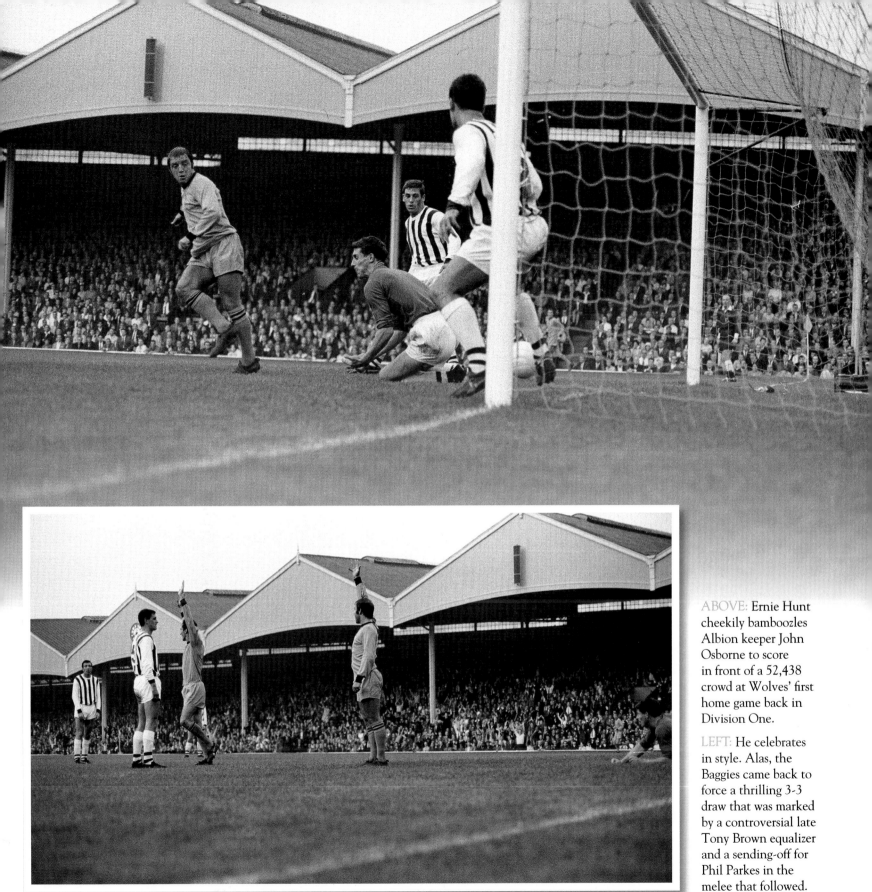

ABOVE: Ernie Hunt cheekily bamboozles Albion keeper John Osborne to score in front of a 52,438 crowd at Wolves' first home game back in Division One.

LEFT: He celebrates in style. Alas, the Baggies came back to force a thrilling 3-3 draw that was marked by a controversial late Tony Brown equalizer and a sending-off for Phil Parkes in the melee that followed.

Excuse me, has he paid for that seat? A sign of the times amid the 1960s hooliganism outbreak came when these Wolves supporters had a guard dog for company as they set off for a Division One match at Manchester City. Alsatians Khyber and Bill had a day out with a fleet of 18 Don Everall coaches destined for Maine Road.

Wolves kept their heads above water in their first season back among the elite, their rise to a final placing of 17th being helped by this 2-0 mid-March victory at Arsenal, where Dave Woodfield is seen being fouled by George Graham. On the left, in Gunners colours, is Bobby Gould – who was later to have two prolific spells at Molineux.

ABOVE: Not what it may seem... the disconsolate figure in the background is not a Wolves player but an opponent from Hull City, as a white-clad Wanderers side, by now under the more disciplinarian management of Bill McGarry, progress to a 3-1 FA Cup third-round victory at Boothferry Park in January 1969. The number 10 with most to celebrate after scoring is Frank Wignall, with two-goal Derek Dougan (left) and winger Mike Kenning also demonstrating their pleasure.

RIGHT: Bobby Thomson, the speedy, stylish England full-back who played 299 matches for Wolves, before being reunited with Stan Cullis, at Birmingham City, in 1969.

116

Where fact is stranger than fiction

You could barely make it up... a fun-loving, hero-worshipped footballer with the world at his feet gives up the goals, the girls and the glory for his religion.

Peter Knowles was a huge favourite at Wolverhampton Wanderers; a similarly coiffured superstar in The Beatles era, and the darling of the North Bank. He had played for England under-23s and was widely expected to challenge strongly for a place in Alf Ramsey's senior squad for the 1970 World Cup finals in Mexico. But he sacrificed it all to pursue his beliefs as a Jehovah's Witness.

Knowles sensationally quit the game in September 1969, although Wolves were so sure he would return that they hung his kit on his peg the following Monday and listed him in their programme for many years on their list of retained players. He was true to his word, though, and stayed away. What's more, through decades of combining work at the Wolverhampton branch of Marks and Spencer with his religion, he has never regretted his momentous decision for a minute.

Knocker doing what he did best

Knowles in the guise in which Wolves fans remember him – wheeling away in an extravagant celebration of scoring, this time against Southampton early in 1969–70. It was the last but one of his 64 goals for the club – a tally compiled in only 191 games.

All eyes are on Peter Knowles as he runs out for his final game – at home to Nottingham Forest on 6th September 1969.

Football idol Peter starts his new life

HIS football career behind him, Peter Knowles arrives at Kingdom Hall, Wolverhampton, yesterday with his wife Jean for his first service as a full-time Jehovah's Witness.

Knowles, 23, who was valued, as a footballer, at about £150,000, played his last game for Wolverhampton on Saturday.

By quitting football, he has lost £100 a week plus his £5,000 club house.

Now he and his wife plan to move into a caravan or a flat, and Peter will start work . . . as a part-time window-cleaner.

The Missing Witness —See Page 23.

His work is done... Knowles sprints off at the final whistle of the 3-3 draw, determined to avoid being mobbed. He grew to hate the idolatry.

The last sad farewell

LEFT: "Okay, just one kiss." A fond farewell from an emotional fan amid a mood of public disbelief.

BELOW: This is my life now… Knowles, with his wife Jean and his literature of choice.

"Squeak" in action with West Ham's Clyde Best at Upton Park, a ground where the full-back was once sent off.

–LEGENDS–

Derek Parkin

Derek Parkin's place in Molineux folklore is guaranteed for all time. And he deserves nothing less for his colossal feat of playing 609 first-team matches for the club.

Thirty years on from his departure for Stoke, his tally of appearances remains a Wolves record and, with the increasing habit of players to move on rather than remain loyal to one shirt, it's difficult to imagine the figure ever being beaten. Parkin's total might have been considerably higher still because he spent several seasons in the full-back academy that was Huddersfield Town before his arrival in the West Midlands on Valentine's Day of 1968. He also missed several months' football in 1972–73 with a suspected heart defect.

Almost 70 games with the Terriers, who were also served in that decade by the likes of Bob McNab, Chris Cattlin and England's World Cup winning left-back Ray Wilson, convinced Ronnie Allen to invest £80,000 of Wolves' money in him. It was a record investment then for a full-back in this country but what excellent value the player proved to be.

In the league alone, he appeared in more than 500 Wanderers matches, and also played in victorious teams in the League Cup finals of 1974 and 1980 as well as in FA Cup semi-finals, a title-winning Division Two side and in much of the run to the 1972 UEFA Cup final.

Parkin, nicknamed "Squeak", won England under-23 honours, represented the Football League and was part of Alf Ramsey's senior squad, most notably in a European Championship qualifier in Malta in 1971. But many sound judges believe he would have won full international caps had he remained in his natural position of right-back rather than being switched by Allen's successor Bill McGarry to the number 3 role.

Such was the Geordie's consistency, even approaching his mid-30s, that he was taken to Stoke in 1982 by Richie Barker, a man who had served as assistant at Molineux to John Barnwell.

Among the plethora of more obscure pieces of history "Squeak" established are ever-present records in 1968–69 and 1969–70 and the playing of 50 or more matches in five different seasons.

FOOTBALL –STATS–

Derek Parkin

Name: Derek Parkin
Born: Newcastle-upon-Tyne 1948
Signed: 1968, from Huddersfield
Playing career: 1964–1983
Clubs: Huddersfield Town, Wolverhampton Wanderers, Stoke City
Wolves appearances: 609
Wolves goals: 10
Football League XI appearances: 1
League Cup winner 1973–74 and 1979–80, UEFA Cup finalist 1971–72, Division Two winner 1976–77

The travails of the Doog

RIGHT: Ref, you might at least wait until I'm on my feet. A vulnerable-looking Derek Dougan is admonished at Stamford Bridge, with Peter Osgood waiting to have his say.

BELOW: Trouble followed the Doog around in 1969–70. Already sent off at Sheffield Wednesday, he went the same way a few weeks later in this home defeat against Everton, which brought two goals for number 10 Hugh Curran and unsavoury crowd scenes.

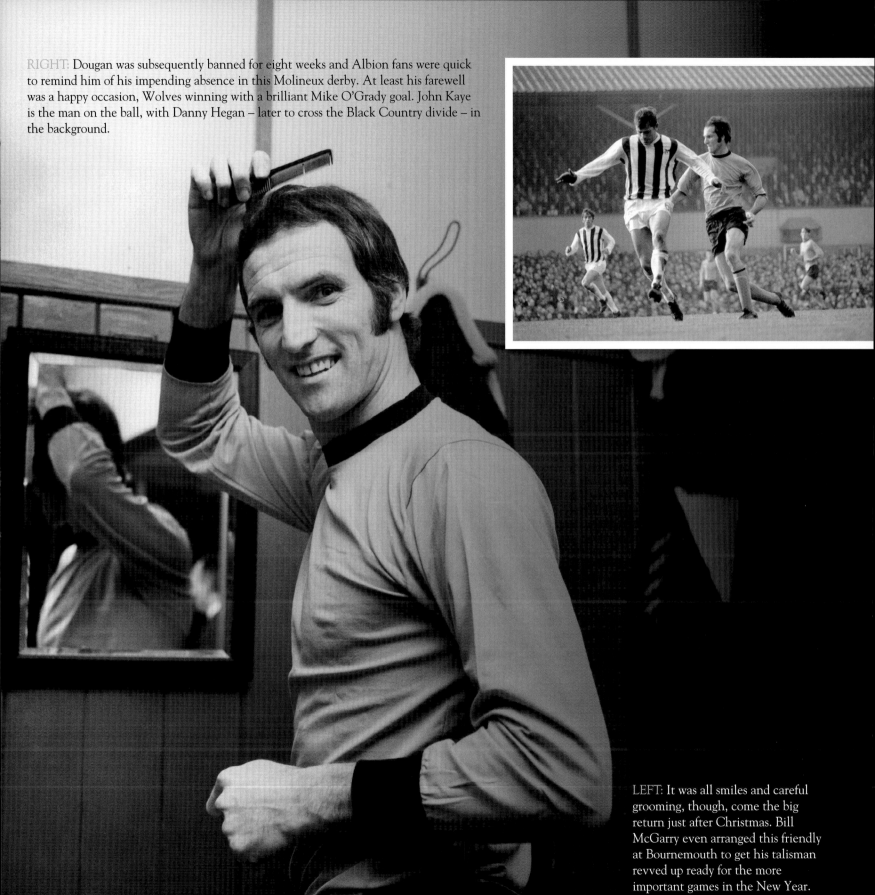

RIGHT: Dougan was subsequently banned for eight weeks and Albion fans were quick to remind him of his impending absence in this Molineux derby. At least his farewell was a happy occasion, Wolves winning with a brilliant Mike O'Grady goal. John Kaye is the man on the ball, with Danny Hegan – later to cross the Black Country divide – in the background.

LEFT: It was all smiles and careful grooming, though, come the big return just after Christmas. Bill McGarry even arranged this friendly at Bournemouth to get his talisman revved up ready for the more important games in the New Year.

A study in unusual shapes as the bent-over Ian Bowyer tries a header at Wolves goal at Maine Road in the late 1960s. The Wanderers players, from left to right, are Gerry Taylor, Frank Munro, John Holsgrove and Manchester-born Les Wilson.

A new type of wall

Dave Wagstaffe finds the taking of a corner delayed as crowd disorder results in police leading a fan out from the packed North Bank. Outbreaks of trouble were an unwanted feature of the game in the late 1960s and 1970s.

Ronnie Allen found a fat cigar and an even fatter salary handsome consolation for being sacked as boss at Molineux, as he moved on to Athletic Bilbao.

Peter Knowles had little interest in materialistic gains by now but was happy to oblige these eager youngsters with the benefit of his knowledge.

Did they really play in that…?

Skipper Mike Bailey goes slip-sliding on an ice-bound Molineux surface in a victory over Sunderland that had repercussions far beyond Wolverhampton and Wearside. The game was the first to be shown live on TV in Scandinavia, so the ranks of the huge gold-and-black army were swelled in big numbers from across the North Sea.

... and this?

Neither keeper John Oldfield, nor his entire back four of Bernard Shaw, Frank Munro, John Holsgrove and Derek Parkin, can prevent Stoke's Denis Smith scoring on this white carpet of a Victoria Ground pitch on Valentine's Day 1970. Hugh Curran's equalizer earned Wolves a point.

A Seventies Surge
1970-1981

Confident smiles from Wolves players before the start of a highly successful 1970–71 season, in which they would finish fourth and qualify for the new UEFA Cup competition. On the far right of the back row is John Richards, who had made his senior debut the previous March, while Danny Hegan (front row, far left) and Bobby Gould (two along from coach Sammy Chung) were two more recent arrivals, in their case via the transfer market.

1970 Kenny Hibbitt scores his first Wolves goal (in a 2-2 draw at Chelsea); John Richards nets his first league goal for Wolves when sent on in a 3-1 win over Huddersfield. 1971 Wolves lift the Texaco Cup by winning 3-1 at Hearts and losing 1-0 in the second leg; Wolves play their first UEFA Cup game and beat Académica de Coimbra 3-0 at Molineux; with all five goals coming in a second half marked by heavy snow, Wolves thrash Arsenal 5-1. 1972 Wolves beat Juventus at Molineux in the UEFA Cup quarter-final after drawing the away leg; McGarry's men narrowly lose an anti-climax of a UEFA Cup final after beating Ferencváros in the semis; Wolves deny Leeds the double by defeating them in a controversial title decider; Wolves lose to their bogey side Spurs in the League Cup semi-final. 1973 Wolves defeat Coventry in the FA Cup quarter-final, only to then be ko'd by Leeds. 1974 Wolves edge past Norwich in the League Cup semi-final; the League Cup comes to Molineux for the first time after Wolves beat Manchester City 2-1 in the final; Wolves return to Europe but lose gallantly to Porto. 1975 Derek Dougan plays his final Wolves game in the 1-1 home draw against Leeds. 1976 Liverpool win 3-1 at Molineux in a title and relegation decider. 1977 Wolves clinch promotion back to the top flight with a 0-0 draw at Plymouth; a side now managed by Sammy Chung then secure the Division Two title with a 1-1 home draw against Chelsea; Wolves deny Bolton promotion with a 1-0 last-day win at Burnden Park and Nottingham Forest go up instead. 1979 Wolves lose 2-0 to Arsenal in the FA Cup semi-final; Andy Gray signs for Wolves on the Molineux pitch and becomes Britain's record signing; Gray makes a goalscoring Wolves debut in a 3-2 win at Everton. 1980 Wolves hit back to beat Swindon in the League Cup semi-final; Wolves beat Nottingham Forest in the League Cup final at Wembley; John Barnwell is now in charge and sees Wolves lose to PSV Eindhoven in the UEFA Cup (the club's last game in Europe). 1981 Wolves beat Middlesbrough in the FA Cup quarter-final in front of Molineux's last 40,000-plus crowd; Wolves lose to Tottenham in the FA Cup semi-final.

Trouble brews for Wolves as George Best prepares to crash a shot at their goal at Old Trafford in April 1971. The Manchester United legend had a boyhood soft spot for Molineux and filled scrapbooks with the club's deeds. Much to the relief of Mike Bailey (left) and John McAlle, this effort came to nothing, but Alan Gowling did hit the only goal to floor a side who had completed a tremendous double by winning at defending league champions Everton two days earlier.

It's McAlle v Man U again, with the Liverpudlian this time thrusting out a long leg at Molineux to halt Brian Kidd's progress. The young defender had dislodged John Holsgrove and would play no fewer than 508 times for the club – a haul of games that is bettered by only five players.

McAlle's centre-half partner for much of the 1970s was Frank Munro, pictured here against one of his former clubs, Chelsea. Munro, whose death in 2011 was widely mourned among his former team-mates and fans, was purchased by Wolves after scoring a hat-trick against them for Aberdeen (aka the Washington Whips) in the 1967 United States tournament.

—LEGENDS—

David Wagstaffe

Wingers had much to live up to at Wolverhampton Wanderers in the 1960s and 1970s.

Following the halcyon years of Johnny Hancocks, Jimmy Mullen and Norman Deeley – all three of them England internationals – it would have been easy for their successors to be viewed as a distinct case of second best.

But the likes of Terry Wharton, Chris Crowe and Alan Hinton were outstanding performers in their own right, then David Wagstaffe came along in their slipstream and proved himself very much up to the mark.

"Waggy" was different in many ways; he frequently disappeared for a crafty cigarette when the manager was about to deliver his team talk and he was always nervous about trips to the theatre and cinema unless he could sit on the end of a row with an escape route in sight.

Even the manner of his Molineux arrival was unusual. He was signed by manager Andy Beattie on Boxing Day morning and made his first appearance for the club (at home to Aston Villa) on the same day that Peter Broadbent made his 497th and last.

He had previously experienced an 8-1 defeat at the ground during one of his 161 games for Manchester City and suffered relegation in his first few months with Wolves. He was a big success as the club came back at the second attempt, though, and made the left-wing position his own for more than a decade, thrilling a generation of Wanderers fans with his dashing runs and brilliant crosses.

No less an authority than Derek Dougan regarded it as an injustice that Wagstaffe remained uncapped by England, although he was called up at schoolboy and youth level and represented the Football League.

In the eyes of the club's supporters, Wagstaffe had nothing to prove as he played and scored in a UEFA Cup final and defied injury to play against his former club in Wolves' 1974 League Cup final victory on his way to a final appearance total of 404.

He later returned to the club to run a bar bearing his name and has in recent years written his own highly entertaining autobiography.

FOOTBALL —STATS—

David Wagstaffe

Name: David Wagstaffe
Born: Manchester 1943
Signed: 1964, from Manchester City
Playing career: 1960–1979
Clubs: Manchester City, Wolverhampton Wanderers, Blackburn Rovers, Blackpool, Blackburn Rovers
Wolves appearances: 404
Wolves goals: 32
Football League XI appearances: 1
League Cup winner 1973–74, UEFA Cup finalist 1971–72

Derek Dougan leads a training ground exercise in the build-up to Wolves' UEFA Cup return at home to Carl Zeiss Jena in December 1971. The striker scored nine goals in that Euro campaign and remains the club's leading all-time scorer in European competition.

Hitting the heights

Another goal for the Doog, this time at Old Trafford on a memorable January afternoon in 1972 when Wolves led Manchester United 3-0 and had their fans chanting "easy, easy" before coasting to a 3-1 victory. John Richards, on target himself soon afterwards, readies himself for a possible loose ball.

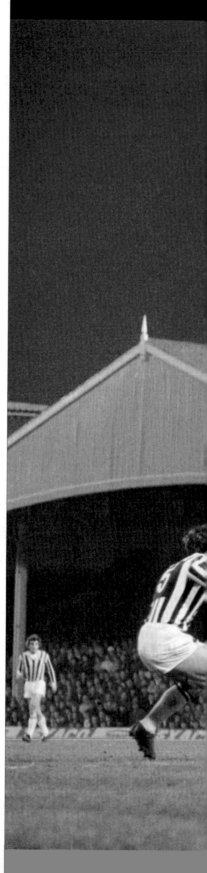

Two days after Old Trafford... a trip to face the powers that be. Dave Wagstaffe (left) and Jim McCalliog (one in from the right) await the verdict after appearing at a disciplinary hearing at London's Great Western Hotel to appeal against bookings received in a game with Coventry. Derek Dougan, present in his role as chairman of the PFA, looks confident, chairman John Ireland (far right) considerably less so, while manager Bill McGarry is perhaps somewhere in-between. The Doog was partially successful with his "Blarney" – McCalliog's appeal failed but Wagstaffe was successful in his.

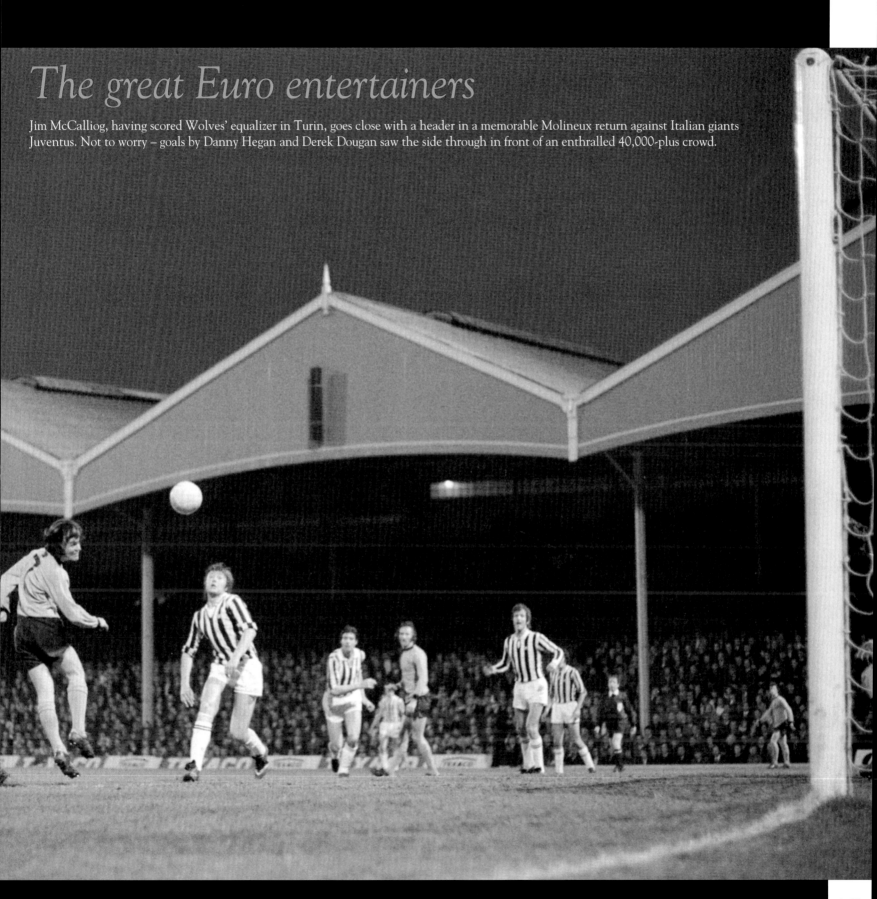

The great Euro entertainers

Jim McCalliog, having scored Wolves' equalizer in Turin, goes close with a header in a memorable Molineux return against Italian giants Juventus. Not to worry – goals by Danny Hegan and Derek Dougan saw the side through in front of an enthralled 40,000-plus crowd.

The only letdown for Wolves in their European adventure was that they didn't even need their passports for the final. Tottenham Hotspur were their opponents over two games in May 1972, and prevailed by the odd goal, thanks largely to a 2-1 first-leg win in the West Midlands. The Doog, whose nine goals in the competition had equalled a British scoring record in a European campaign, battles here with Mike England.

UEFA Cup final 1972

First leg:

Date & Venue: 3rd May 1972 at Molineux.

Result: Wolves (0) 1 Tottenham Hotspur (0) 2.

Wolves: Parkes, Shaw, Taylor, Hegan, Munro, McAlle, McCalliog, Hibbitt, Richards, Dougan, Wagstaffe. Subs: Parkin, Arnold, Curran, Daley, Eastoe.

Tottenham Hotspur: Jennings, Kinnear, Knowles, Mullery, England, Beal, Gilzean, Perryman, Chivers, Peters, Coates (Pratt). Subs: Evans, Daines, Naylor, Pearce.

Goals: Chivers (57 min), McCalliog (72 min), Chivers (87 min).

Attendance: 38,362.

Second leg:

Date & Venue: 17th May 1972 at White Hart Lane.

Result: Tottenham Hotspur (1) 1 Wolves (1) 1 (Aggregate 3-2).

Tottenham Hotspur: Jennings, Kinnear, Knowles, Mullery, England, Beal, Gilzean, Perryman, Chivers, Peters, Coates. Subs: Evans, Daines, Naylor, Pratt, Pearce.

Wolves: Parkes, Shaw, Taylor, Hegan, Munro, McAlle, McCalliog, Hibbitt (Bailey), Richards, Dougan (Curran), Wagstaffe. Subs: Parkin, Arnold, Daley.

Goals: Mullery (29 min), Wagstaffe (40 min).

Attendance: 54,303.

Captain: Jim McCalliog.

Manager: Bill McGarry.

The key moment from the White Hart Lane return as Alan Mullery nips in ahead of Phil Parkes to nod in Spurs' goal. Although Dave Wagstaffe equalized spectacularly, Wolves couldn't quite repair the damage and had to stick to domestic travelling the following season.

At least Wolves ended their league campaign on a memorable note in front of an enthralled 53,379 crowd at Molineux. They beat Leeds United 2-1 and so denied the FA Cup winners the single point they needed to secure the double. It meant a sad exit at full-time for Leeds skipper Billy Bremner.

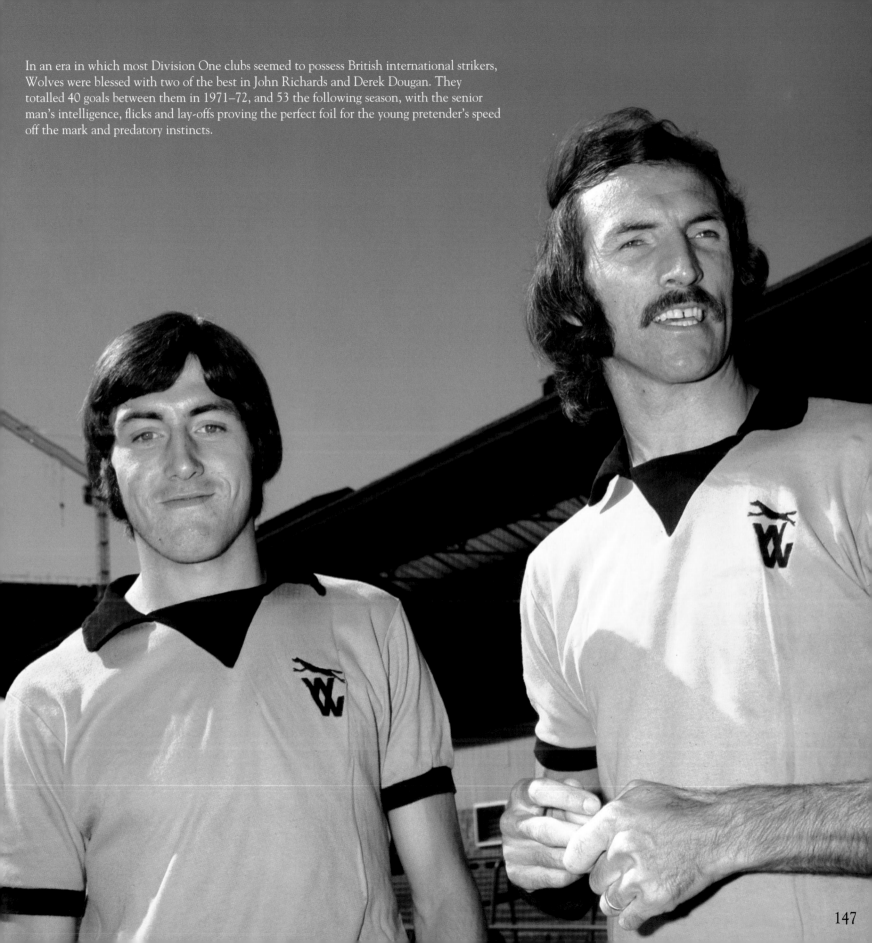

In an era in which most Division One clubs seemed to possess British international strikers, Wolves were blessed with two of the best in John Richards and Derek Dougan. They totalled 40 goals between them in 1971–72, and 53 the following season, with the senior man's intelligence, flicks and lay-offs proving the perfect foil for the young pretender's speed off the mark and predatory instincts.

147

Another match made in heaven for Richards... the off-field relationship with girlfriend Pam that became a long and happy marriage.

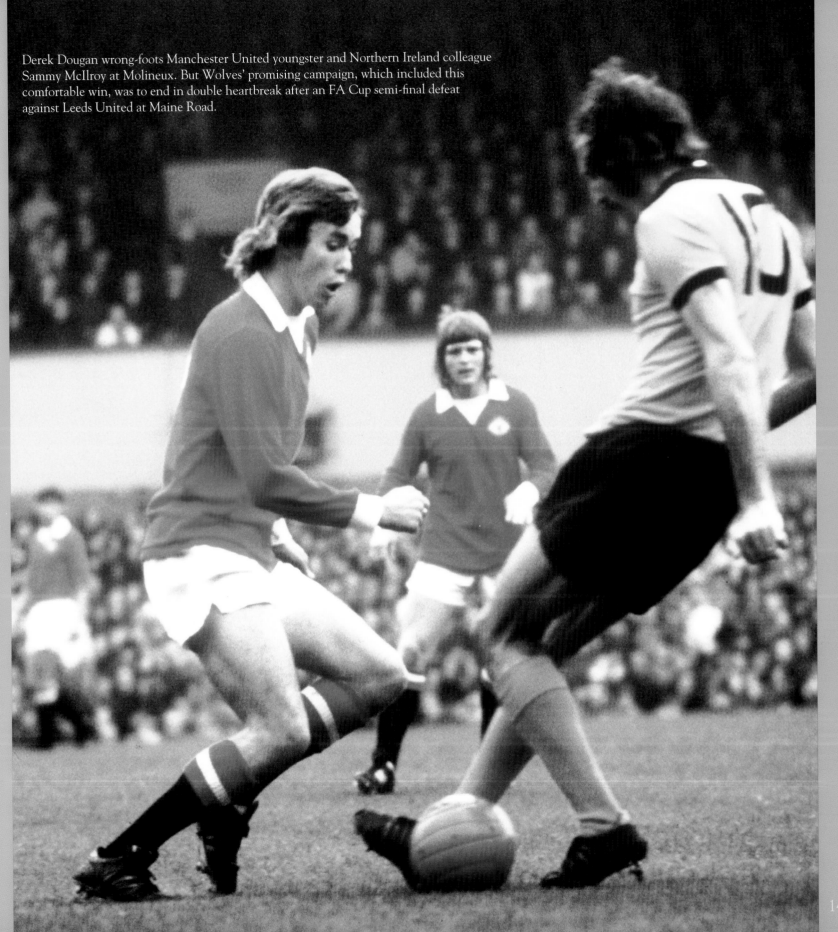

Derek Dougan wrong-foots Manchester United youngster and Northern Ireland colleague Sammy McIlroy at Molineux. But Wolves' promising campaign, which included this comfortable win, was to end in double heartbreak after an FA Cup semi-final defeat against Leeds United at Maine Road.

A dress rehearsal for '74?

Another successful Molineux season was under way by the time Wolves travelled to
Manchester City in 1972–73 and took a point from a 1-1 draw, in which John McAlle had
to keep a close eye on Rodney Marsh. Bill McGarry's side had recovered from two opening
defeats and would finish fifth in the table.

The curse of Spurs strikes again

Seven months after the UEFA Cup final heartbreak, Wolves were defeated by the odd goal by the same opponents in the semi-final of the League Cup. Kenny Hibbitt gives his side hope by beating Pat Jennings with a penalty at Molineux but the first-leg score was depressingly familiar and Tottenham clung to their 2-1 lead by hitting back to draw the return 2-2 after extra-time.

White Heartbreak Lane

The pose of keeper Phil Parkes and full-back Bernard Shaw say everything as a young home fan runs on to the Spurs pitch in celebration.

John Richards moves menacingly away from Coventry City's Bobby Parker on the day goals by he and Kenny Hibbitt settled the all-Midlands FA Cup quarter-final in 1973. Behind Richards is Willie Carr, the midfielder who later moved to Molineux. More than 50,000 were present but the day started badly for Wolves, with Derek Dougan poleaxed in the pre-match warm-up by a wayward shot from substitute Steve Kindon and at one stage in danger of being sidelined.

Billy Bremner, a disconsolate figure when trooping off Molineux the previous spring, on an altogether happier occasion for him – the FA Cup semi-final at Manchester City, where he drove in the winning goal. Wolves weren't alone in the near-miss stakes. Leeds lost in the final to Division Two Sunderland.

Frank Munro, an imperious presence in Wolves' side for nearly a decade.

Two of the young faces in Wolves' historic 1973–74 campaign; full-back Geoff Palmer (left), whose debut had come in a win at Arsenal in a now-defunct fixture – the play-off for third and fourth places in the FA Cup – and midfielder Barry Powell. Both were to be part of a special day for Wolves several months later.

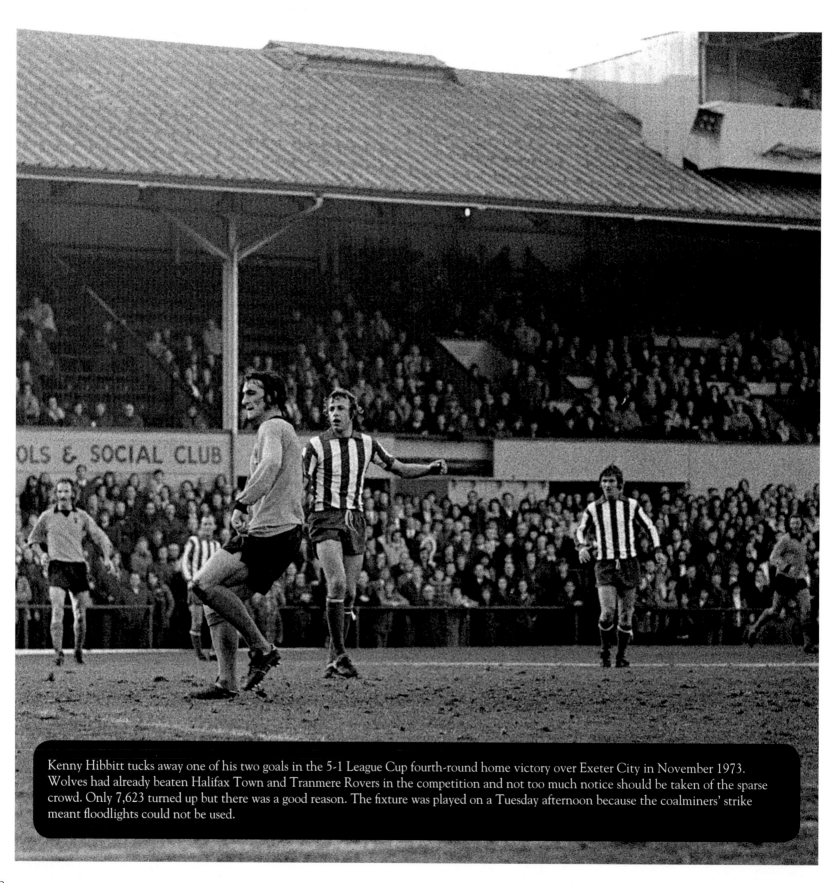

Kenny Hibbitt tucks away one of his two goals in the 5-1 League Cup fourth-round home victory over Exeter City in November 1973. Wolves had already beaten Halifax Town and Tranmere Rovers in the competition and not too much notice should be taken of the sparse crowd. Only 7,623 turned up but there was a good reason. The fixture was played on a Tuesday afternoon because the coalminers' strike meant floodlights could not be used.

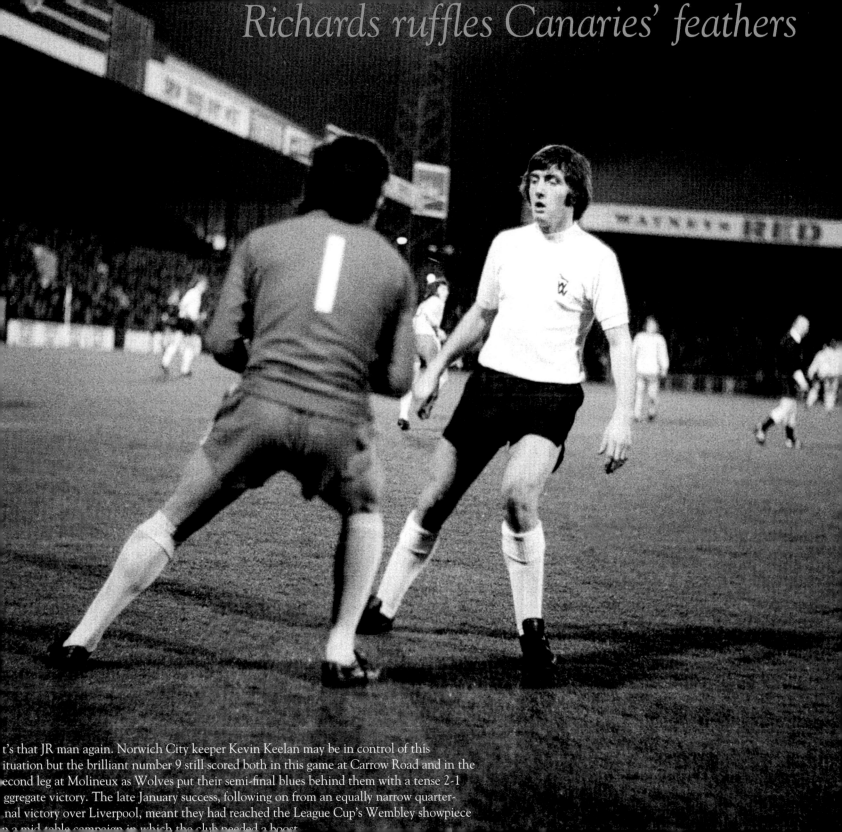

t's that JR man again. Norwich City keeper Kevin Keelan may be in control of this
ituation but the brilliant number 9 still scored both in this game at Carrow Road and in the
econd leg at Molineux as Wolves put their semi-final blues behind them with a tense 2-1
ggregate victory. The late January success, following on from an equally narrow quarter-
nal victory over Liverpool, meant they had reached the League Cup's Wembley showpiece
n a mid-table campaign in which the club needed a boost.

Rocking Wembley once more

That'll do nicely for starters. Kenny Hibbitt runs away in celebration of the right-foot volley that arced away from Manchester City keeper Keith MacRae to open the scoring shortly before half-time. The finish clearly met with the approval of former City winger Dave Wagstaffe, who kept a hamstring injury secret from Bill McGarry in case the manager left him out.

League Cup final 1974

Date & Venue: 2nd March 1974 at Wembley.

Result: Wolves (1) 2 Manchester City (0) 1.

Wolves: Pierce, Palmer, Parkin, Bailey, Munro, McAlle, Hibbitt, Sunderland, Richards, Dougan, Wagstaffe (Powell).

Manchester City: MacRae, Pardoe, Donachie, Doyle, Booth, Towers, Summerbee, Bell, Lee, Law, Marsh (Carrodus).

Goals: Hibbitt (43 min), Bell (53 min), Richards (85 min).

Attendance: 97,886.

Captain: Mike Bailey.

Manager: Bill McGarry.

The story of Wembley '74 as far as many Wolves fans are concerned. Gary Pierce flies across his goal to produce one of several fine saves to frustrate City's star-studded forward line. And all that on the keeper's 23rd birthday – one that ended with a "man hug" from an ecstatic McGarry.

161

Get in, you beauty!

John Richards flashes Alan Sunderland's deflected pull-back past City defenders Mike Doyle and Tommy Booth for Wolves' Wembley winner. Only five minutes remained when the one-cap England international, watched by Derek Dougan, struck his seventh and most famous League Cup goal of 1973–74.

A tender moment between two colourful veterans…
Denis Law, having already exchanged shirts with
his Scottish international colleague Frank Munro,
sportingly manages a grin during this embrace from
Derek Dougan. It was the first major medal of Dougan's
long career and made this occasion a world away from
his previous cup final appearance, in 1960.

The celebrations begin as Wolves players pose with the cup after descending the famous steps. In the tracksuit on the left is Dave Wagstaffe, who eventually succumbed to his injury. John Richards had also been struggling but somehow completed what was his only match that season after a game at Everton on the 9th of February.

Something nice and new for the cabinet

The moment Mike Bailey described as "shivery" – the raising of Wolves' first major silverware for 14 years. The club had won the Texaco Cup in 1971 but this was something else altogether. McGarry, tired of all the near misses, had privately told himself he would quit if his side had been pipped at the post yet again. Now, he had another European campaign to plan for.

–LEGENDS–

Mike Bailey

What Wolverhampton Wanderers would have given for a few more years of this inspirational character at his peak! Mike Bailey had already won two England caps (sadly, the only two he was destined to win) when Ronnie Allen's flair for spotting a bargain hauled him in during the club's 1965–66 Division Two season.

Cambridgeshire-born Bailey cut his teeth in professional football at Charlton, impressing for the Londoners against Wolves, before being recruited to Molineux as a 24-year-old. And it didn't take him long to be made captain at his new club – a role he held for around a decade.

The barrel-chested midfielder skippered the side to promotion in his first full season at Molineux and was named Midland Footballer of the Year in the process. He soon proved himself a good foil to the likes of the more attack-minded Peter Knowles and David Burnside as Ron Flowers' phenomenal career drew towards a close.

Injury then meant Bailey joined late when Wolves contested and won the seven-week-long United Soccer Association Championship, using Los Angeles as their base and even prefixing their name to that of California's most colourful city.

He was an even more valuable servant after Bill McGarry had replaced Allen in 1968, continuing to oversee consolidation back in the top flight and leading from the front as the club then became a major force in the game.

Under his captaincy, the club lifted the Texaco Cup and finished fourth in Division One in 1970–71. But there was disappointment the following season when injury sidelined him for the second half of the run to the final of the inaugural UEFA Cup, although he returned as a substitute at Tottenham for the second leg at that last stage.

Bailey, who also won England under-23 recognition, helped Wolves to the semi-final of both domestic cups in 1972–73 and finally got his hands on some major silverware when he was first up Wembley's famous steps following the League Cup final victory over Manchester City in 1974.

He departed for America two years later and subsequently embarked on a substantial career in coaching, management and scouting.

FOOTBALL –STATS–

Mike Bailey

Name: Mike Bailey
Born: Wisbech 1942
Signed: 1966, from Charlton
Playing career: 1958–1979
Clubs: Charlton Athletic, Wolverhampton Wanderers, Minnesota Kicks, Hereford United
Wolves appearances: 436
Wolves goals: 25
England appearances: 2
Football League XI appearances: 3
League Cup winner 1973–74, UEFA Cup finalist 1971–72, Division Two winner 1976–77 (played 10 games)

–LEGENDS–

John Richards

From a time when record books to acknowledge such feats were few and far between, John Richards stood proud for well over a decade as Wolves' highest ever goalscorer.

His feat of netting for the 171st time and eclipsing Billy Hartill as the club's record marksman went largely unheralded – at least compared with the accolades that Steve Bull received when he overtook Richards in March 1992.

The skinhead striker would go on to finish with 306 Wolves goals but 1970s Molineux diehards might argue that the vast majority of Richards' final total of 194 came in the top division.

The player was picked up by the club from the rugby league stronghold of Warrington when he impressed in a schools tournament at Bognor Regis, making his debut in a Black Country derby at West Brom in February 1970, but having to wait another seven months for his first league goal.

Once he had secured a regular first-team shirt alongside Derek Dougan at the expense of Bobby Gould and Hugh Curran, there was no holding him. He scored 16 goals in 1971–72 and more than doubled the total 12 months later as he made himself the country's top marksman for the season.

The heroics in the number 9 shirt earned him full England recognition on top of his various schoolboy, under-21 and under-23 honours; alas, he only won a solitary senior cap – playing wide on the left against Northern Ireland at Goodison Park in the 1973 Home Championship.

His proudest moment came the following March when he struck the late winner against Manchester City in the first of his two League Cup finals with Wolves. He also netted home and away in the semi-final against Norwich and struck a beauty in a losing cause in the 1972–73 semi-final against Tottenham.

Having later clicked with Andy Gray, it's no surprise Richards holds the honour of being the club's highest scorer in the League Cup. He also tops their FA Cup goals list and, for good measure, struck the equalizer against Chelsea in 1977 that secured the Division Two title. From 1997 to 2000, he served as the club's managing director in a six-year stint on the board.

FOOTBALL
–STATS–

John Richards

Name: John Richards
Born: Warrington 1950
Signed: 1967, as a trainee
Playing career: 1967–1984
Clubs: Wolverhampton Wanderers, Derby County (loan), Maritimo
Wolves appearances: 485
Wolves goals: 194

England appearances: 1

Football League XI appearances: 1

League Cup winner 1973–74 and 1979–80, UEFA Cup finalist 1971–72, Division Two winner 1976–77

Goodbye *to the* Pied Piper

Vintage Doog! As if to underline the point that there was no one better at "playing" the crowd, the man of the moment finds himself with a sizeable entourage as he embarks on his lap of honour, starting, of course, in front of his adoring North Bank.

–LEGENDS–

Derek Dougan

Charismatic and flamboyant, Derek Dougan nevertheless bounced into Molineux as a football journeyman: a rangy talent who had seemed to spend his entire career on the move. In Wolverhampton, close to his 30th birthday, he found a spiritual home.

Having been at seven clubs in ten years, the Belfast-born centre-forward spent the next eight and a half seasons in the West Midlands, endearing himself to a new public and delivering goals in abundance. In a post-1966 era in which the game was becoming more defensive, the Doog netted 123 times in 323 first-team appearances and formed a terrific partnership with John Richards. Initially, he helped the club over the finishing line in their 1966–67 Division Two promotion-winning campaign and then to consolidation back in the top flight.

His golden season, though, was 1971–72, when he was not only Bill McGarry's top league marksman with 15 but able to add nine in a UEFA Cup campaign that ended in a two-leg defeat against Tottenham in the final. The haul made him Wolves' all-time highest scorer in Europe. Not bad for a player who didn't get on with that particular disciplinarian manager!

Dougan was Molineux's great Pied Piper. He had a magnetic personality and gift of the gab that made him much more than a player and, as the TV, radio and PFA work rolled in, he showed a common touch by being a hero to thousands of impressionable youngsters.

Presented with a League Cup winner's medal as the swansong to his long playing career, he lived up to his reputation as a photographer's best friend by standing in the crowd at the first match after he had helped save the club from extinction in 1982. Only three minutes were left before a Friday 5pm deadline when he stepped in at the start of a reign that was sadly nothing like as successful as the one he had on the pitch.

The Doog was box office. He could be controversial and contrary and he was always highly opinionated, but Molineux would have been a much duller place without him and would not have witnessed so many memorable days and nights.

FOOTBALL –STATS–

Derek Dougan

Name: Derek Dougan
Born: Belfast 1938

Died: 2007
Signed: 1967, from Leicester
Playing career: 1957–1977
Clubs: Distillery, Portsmouth, Blackburn Rovers, Aston Villa, Peterborough United, Leicester City, Wolverhampton Wanderers, Kettering Town
Wolves appearances: 323
Wolves goals: 123

Northern Ireland appearances: 43

League Cup winner 1973–74, UEFA Cup finalist 1971–72

Willie Carr, whose Wolves debut had been an extraordinary 7-1 triumph over Chelsea five months earlier, is harassed by fellow Scottish international Lou Macari on the opening day of 1975–76. Manchester United won 2-0 to set the tone for a difficult and ultimately heartbreaking Molineux campaign.

Don't be fooled... this premature Molineux pitch invasion had nothing to do with Wolves fans. All the celebrations were on the side of visiting Liverpool as they set up the victory they needed to earn them a ninth title. In what was billed on the front cover of the match programme as "the great First Division drama", McGarry's men needed to win and Birmingham City lose at Sheffield United on the same night for Wolves to survive. At half-time, after Steve Kindon's early goal, things were working out, but Liverpool struck three times in the final 13 minutes to condemn their hosts to relegation barely two years after the winning of the League Cup. McGarry paid for the drop with his job.

Haven't we met before?

Wolves' one-year stay back in Division Two soon brought them into contact with two adversaries from grander stages. In their goalless draw at Fulham in September 1976 they had to keep a close eye on George Best and Rodney Marsh – a task carried out here by Steve Daley and number 11 Alan Sunderland. The gold-shirted duo were among five players who scored 10 goals or more as Wolves bounced back as champions.

LEFT: Bob Hazell and George Berry – two of the new kids on the block in the second half of the 1970s as Wolves looked to replace Frank Munro and, considerably later, John McAlle. The veteran duo played 879 games for the club between them.

BELOW: Tense moments for a Wolves side who consolidated under Sammy Chung back in the top flight in 1977–78 and then reached this FA Cup semi-final against Arsenal the following season. John Barnwell was now in charge and saw his side beaten 2-0 at Villa Park, former Molineux favourite Alan Sunderland scoring one of the goals.

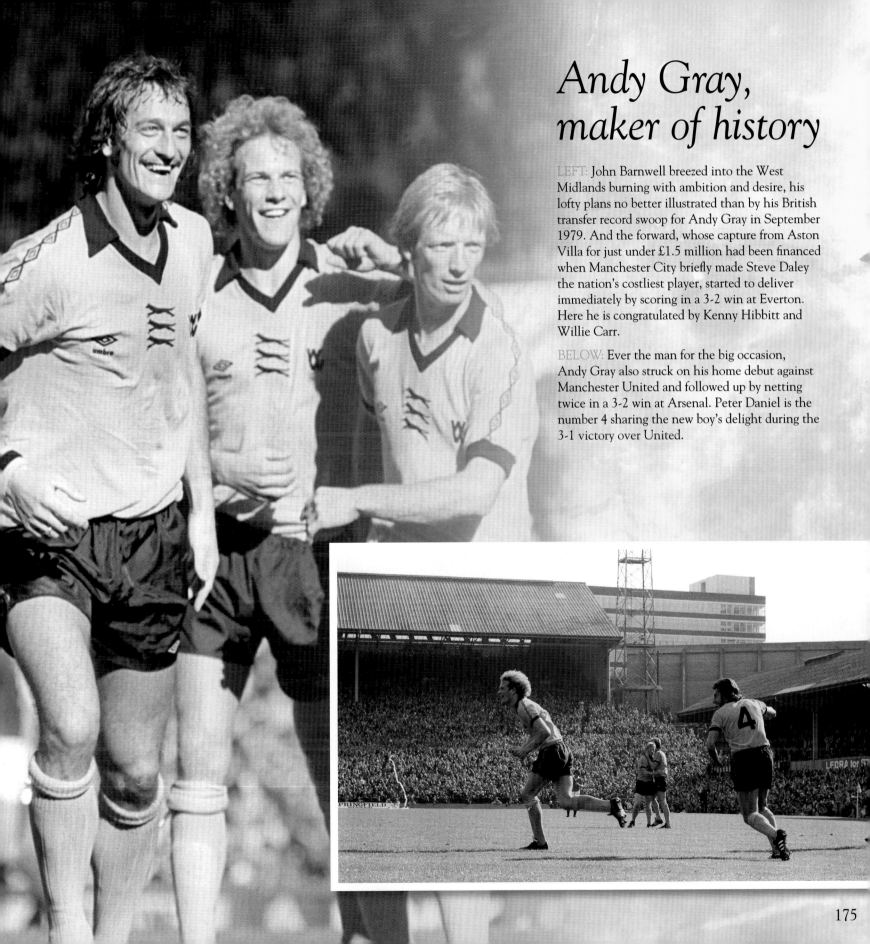

Andy Gray, maker of history

LEFT: John Barnwell breezed into the West Midlands burning with ambition and desire, his lofty plans no better illustrated than by his British transfer record swoop for Andy Gray in September 1979. And the forward, whose capture from Aston Villa for just under £1.5 million had been financed when Manchester City briefly made Steve Daley the nation's costliest player, started to deliver immediately by scoring in a 3-2 win at Everton. Here he is congratulated by Kenny Hibbitt and Willie Carr.

BELOW: Ever the man for the big occasion, Andy Gray also struck on his home debut against Manchester United and followed up by netting twice in a 3-2 win at Arsenal. Peter Daniel is the number 4 sharing the new boy's delight during the 3-1 victory over United.

Treading familiar turf

As in 1974, Wolves fans were allocated the tunnel end of Wembley for the final game in a League Cup journey that had accounted for Burnley, Crystal Palace, QPR, Grimsby Town and Swindon Town. The ticket distribution saw to it that the gold and black faithful had the best view when their heroes, led by Emlyn Hughes, emerged before kick-off, alongside hot favourites Nottingham Forest.

In the goalmouths where Gary Pierce had performed heroics six years earlier, Paul Bradshaw worked wonders to defy the side who were reigning European Cup holders and would retain the trophy a few weeks after this all-Midlands clash. The keeper even knocks his team-mate Andy Gray out of the way here to punch clear, while Geoff Palmer guards the line and number 11 Mel Eves prepares for a possible knockdown.

No prizes for guessing who was the match-winner… Andy Gray does his party piece after the simple left-foot tap-in that proved to be the only goal. Gray capitalized on a mix-up between Peter Shilton and David Needham following Peter Daniel's long through ball, and then circumnavigated the cameramen in celebration.

Wembley elation all over again

League Cup final 1980

Date & Venue: 15th March 1980 at Wembley.

Result: Wolves (0) 1 Nottingham Forest (0) 0.

Wolves: Bradshaw, Palmer, Parkin, Daniel, Hughes, Berry, Hibbitt, Carr, Gray, Richards, Eves. Sub: Brazier.

Nottingham Forest: Shilton, Anderson, F Gray, McGovern, Needham, Burns, O'Neill, Bowyer, Birtles, Francis, Robertson. Sub: O'Hare.

Goal: Gray (67 min).

Attendance: 96,527.

Captain: Emlyn Hughes.

Manager: John Barnwell.

Some important grooming for George Berry, a West German-born Welsh international defender, in the latter stages of Wolves' victorious League Cup run. The club had reached the final by pulling back a 2-1 first-leg deficit against Division Three Swindon Town at the last-four stage, "barber" John Richards scoring twice and Mel Eves once to see that the Wiltshire club, unlike Berry's hair, suffered the chop.

Black Country boy Mel Eves celebrates his goal against PSV Eindhoven in Wolves' last major European game. By scoring in the first-round second-leg clash on 1st October 1980, the forward gave his side hope of retrieving a 3-1 deficit suffered in Holland. But they fell a goal short on a night on which a delay caused by floodlit failure checked their momentum.

One for the Hibbitt family scrapbook... Wolves' Kenny does battle with Newcastle United's Terry at Molineux early in 1974. In the same fixture the following season, Kenny hit all four goals – part of the tally of 114 he managed in total for the club and as good a reason as any for Newcastle to have tried to sign him in the late 1970s.

–LEGENDS–

Kenny Hibbitt

FOOTBALL
–STATS–

Kenny Hibbitt

Name: Kenny Hibbitt
Born: Bradford 1951
Signed: 1968, from Bradford
Park Avenue
Playing career: 1967–1988
Clubs: Bradford Park Avenue,
Wolverhampton Wanderers,
Seattle Sounders (loan),
Coventry City, Bristol Rovers
Wolves appearances: 574
Wolves goals: 114
League Cup winner 1973–74
and 1979–80, UEFA Cup
finalist 1971–72, Division
Two winner 1976–77

Only Derek Parkin has played more Wolverhampton Wanderers games than Kenny Hibbitt.

The goalscoring midfielder's tally of 574 league and cup appearances for the club is only 35 shy of his long-time team-mate and not too shabby for a player who cost a mere £5,000 when recruited from Bradford Park Avenue late in 1968!

In another era, Hibbitt would surely have been decorated with England caps, such was his industry, range of passing, and knack for coming up with vital goals.

As it was, all he had to show by way of international recognition was a single appearance for England under-23s – as a substitute against Wales.

He played in an era, though, in which he was competing for a place with the likes of Alan Ball, Gerry Francis and Steve Coppell, and he suggests, three or four decades on, that he was slightly short of that elite class.

Thousands of Wolves fans might question that modest opinion but what pleasure he gave with his explosive shooting. And what a debt Wolves owed Ronnie Allen for recruiting the youngster from his native West Yorkshire.

The manager, who had already built the backbone of an excellent side by signing Mike Bailey, Derek Dougan, Parkin and Frank Munro in cut-price deals, was sacked a day or two after Hibbitt's arrival, so it was Allen's successor Bill McGarry who reaped the rewards of his expert talent-spotting.

Hibbitt, who once scored all four of Wolves' goals in an emphatic Molineux victory over a Newcastle side containing his elder brother Terry, established himself in 1970–71 and struck the opener in the memorable League Cup final win over star-studded Manchester City.

He was still going strong when the club returned to Wembley for another afternoon of glory in the competition six years later, and was given an emotional reception when welcomed back as assistant manager of Bristol Rovers in 1989.

He was linked with a Molineux return as a possible part of Graham Taylor's backroom team in the mid-1990s. Alas, such opportunity ultimately eluded him in his management and coaching career.

Despite some signs of looming financial difficulty, caused by the building of the cavernous John Ireland Stand, Molineux was all smiles when two goals in extra time saw off Middlesbrough in an FA Cup quarter-final replay in March 1981. Kenny Hibbitt is the man struggling to reach the dressing rooms here, following an invasion by the more demonstrative element of the club's last 40,000-plus crowd.

A celebration from afar

Animated celebration from Paul Bradshaw as Willie Carr's controversial late penalty earns Wolves a reprieve in their FA Cup semi-final against Tottenham Hotspur at Hillsborough in 1981. The escape was only temporary, though. A Spurs side, for whom Glenn Hoddle had scored, with a free-kick, in the first meeting, ran out 3-0 winners of the replay at Highbury four nights later.

Almost a Last Stand
1982-1987

The building of what became known as the John Ireland Stand was meant to herald an exciting new era at Molineux. Instead, the financing of it sent Wolverhampton Wanderers hurtling into trouble and close to the abyss.

1982 Relegated Wolves beat Blackburn in the first game after the club emerge from administration. **1983** Wolves draw 3-3 at Charlton to win promotion back to the top division; A 3-1 win at WBA in late November gives out-of-depth Wolves their first league win of the season. **1985** Bill McGarry returns for a second spell as manager. **1986** Wolves arrive in Division Four after a third successive relegation and another lapse into administration; Graham Turner is appointed manager and signs Steve Bull the following month.

Wayne Clarke takes the plaudits from John Richards and Mel Eves following the point-winning goal at Everton that gave Wolves hope in their final away game of 1981–82. Relegation in 21st place was soon confirmed, though, and the club spent most of the summer battling for their very existence.

What a save!

Only three minutes remained before the 5pm deadline when a consortium led by Derek Dougan ensured the survival of Wolverhampton Wanderers in August 1982. The club came out of administration and lived to fight another season. Left to right in this celebratory photo are financial adviser Stewart Ross (an amateur Wolves player in the 1960s), directors Roger Hipkiss and Doug Hope, chairman Doog, general manager Eric Woodward and manager Ian Greaves. The latter's demeanour supports his belief that he and Dougan had too much "previous" to work together. He was right and was quickly replaced with Graham Hawkins.

Wolves unexpectedly won immediate promotion as 1982–83 runners-up to QPR. The impressive progress was especially surprising considering money was tight and the accent was very much on youth. Derek Dougan had stood among the fans on the terraces for the opening victory at home to Blackburn Rovers and was delighted to announce the club's first shirt sponsor deal in the autumn – a happy event for which (from left) John Humphrey, John Pender, John Burridge, Bob Coy and Geoff Palmer were on parade.

Wolves' return to the top flight was little short of a nightmare and they plummeted straight out of it again by finishing bottom. One pre-Christmas highlight was a Danny Crainie-inspired victory at West Brom, while January contained this stunning success at Anfield, where Mark Lawrenson and Alan Hansen are the men in attendance as Wayne Clarke challenges. The hero was Steve Mardenborough (pictured in the background), who scored the only goal against a Liverpool side heading for the title for the third year running.

Even in Division One, six of Wolves' attendances in 1983–84 dipped below 10,000, none more alarmingly than when a paltry 6,611 turned up for this 3-0 defeat against Ipswich Town in April. The club would part with manager Graham Hawkins before their relegation fate was sealed and they were once more on a slippery slope.

BELOW: Molineux's main entrance, as fans of a certain age will affectionately remember it. In the mid-1980s, though, it was hardly a hive of excited match-day activity. And, soon, two sides of a traditionally throbbing, compact ground would be condemned, depriving it of much of its atmosphere.

Bottoming out at last

Wolverhampton Wanderers had another flirtation with oblivion in the summer of 1986 before finally starting the long haul back.

There seemed to be no end to their suffering as they experienced a third successive relegation in 1985–86, a season in which their fall from grace is best illustrated by the fact that they had no fewer than 17 Molineux crowds below 4,000, four of them nosediving under the 3,000 mark.

Amid talk that they might vacate their famous home to ground-share with Birmingham City and Walsall, or even go out of business and reform as a non-league club, they arrived in Division Four for the first time in a summer during which they again lapsed into administration.

At least fans had seen the back, though, of the despised Bhatti regime that Derek Dougan had misguidedly put his name to, and a complicated salvation package was subsequently being thrashed out between the club, Wolverhampton Council, the building company J J Gallagher and supermarket giant Asda.

The Gallagher brothers propped Wolves up while they built a new superstore a goal-kick away from the North Bank and, following the years of neglect, two football-loving directors, Dick Homden and Jack Harris, were installed to make sure things improved on the pitch.

One of their first moves was an unpopular one: the removal of acting manager Brian Little at a time when improvement was already in the air. And his replacement, Graham Turner, had a difficult baptism as Wolves lost as many Division Four matches as they won.

Then, on 20ᵗʰ November 1986, Homden and Harris scraped together £70,000 and Turner took

The Birmingham-based *Evening Mail* portrays the gloom surrounding the lowest point in Wolves' 134-year history – a 3-0 FA Cup defeat against Multipart League club Chorley.

O BY NON LEAGUERS

RIP

ES!

LEON HICKMAN'S
MOLINEUX
REQUIEM

well beaten.

"I am bearing the brunt of four to five years of bad management."

Last week, Wolves bought Steve Bull and Andy Thompson from West Brom for £70,000 and 32-year-old Barry Powell, who was sold to Coventry by the club as a youngster, has re-joined them from Hong Kong.

But to make room for more new players, Turner will have to prune the 23-strong playing staff, probably the biggest outside the First Division. And, evidence now suggests the worst.

The job of Turner and his assistant, Gary Pendrey, now must be to prevent a slither to the bottom of the Fourth Division and from there to six-foot under.

● DEREK LAWRENSON saw the debacle — read his report on Page 35.

and they saved the club on the brink of extinction. They knew the size of the job I had to do.

"It has been the most humiliating night in the history of a great club. All we can do is sit down and analyse what happened — and try to put it right."

"I recognise we are square at the back and that this led to two of Chorley's goals, but that isn't really the point.

"We should beat a team who, when we played them first, were in the lower half of the Multi Part League. It wasn't a 0-1 surprise. We were

the word of his chief scout Ron Jukes, trusted his own eyes and rang West Bromwich Albion manager Ron Saunders to ask if he could buy Andy Thompson and a certain Steve Bull.

Still the team hadn't quite bottomed out and Bull famously turned to Thompson a couple of weeks later and asked "What have we let ourselves in for here, mate?" as they sat together in disbelief at Wolves' 3-0 FA Cup defeat against Multipart League club Chorley.

But enough was enough. Bull took matters into his own hands and finished what was left of that season with 19 Wolves goals. The team won 15 of their final 19 league games and just missed out on automatic promotion.

The fact they then lost to Aldershot in the first ever staging of end-of-season play-offs just seemed to underline the fact that the club were cursed in some way. But the extra 12 months in the basement just served to make sure Turner got it absolutely right in leading them into an intoxicating period of renaissance that bore out the Wolves motto: Out of darkness cometh light.

BELOW: Wolves' journey to two successive titles – and the landmark of becoming the first club to win all four English divisions – started with a headache. Their opening-day 2-2 draw at Neil Warnock's Scarborough, like the previous season's trips to Torquay United and Southend United, was marked by serious crowd disorder.

Beware of the Bull

1988-PRESENT

"Let the Bull loose" became a popular catchphrase, particularly from the lips of Jimmy Greaves, while England were struggling for goals early in their 1990 World Cup finals campaign. And the photographers didn't have to look far for suitable props as they snapped the man who would transform Wolverhampton Wanderers' fortunes.

1988 Wolves beat Burnley to win the Sherpa Van Trophy at Wembley. **1989** Steve Bull makes his international debut, for England under-21s in Albania, and makes a goalscoring senior debut for England in a win away to Scotland; Wolves lose at Middlesbrough in their first game back in Division Two. **1990** Wolves win at Newcastle thanks to four goals by Steve Bull on the first day of the 1990s; "Bully" scores twice at home to Czechoslovakia and subsequently books his place at the Italia 90 World Cup finals. **1992** Steve Bull hits the winner at Derby to become the highest goalscorer in Wolves' history. **1993** Wolves beat Bristol City in the first game at the redeveloped Molineux. **1994** Wolves lose at Chelsea in the FA Cup quarter-final in the final days of Graham Turner's eight-year reign; Wolves win at Bolton in Graham Taylor's first match as manager; Molineux and Wolverhampton come to a standstill in tribute following the death of Billy Wright. **1995** Wolves win an historic penalty shoot-out in an FA Cup tie at home to Sheffield Wednesday; Taylor's Wolves lose in a play-off semi-final second leg at Bolton; a televised draw at home to 10-man Charlton leads to the departure of Graham Taylor. **1997** Wolves lose at Crystal Palace in the play-off semi-finals. **1998** Wolves lose to Arsenal in the FA Cup semi-final after winning at Leeds in the sixth round; a 6-1 win at Bristol City brings a spectacular start to Colin Lee's reign as manager, succeeding his former boss Mark McGhee. **2001** Dave Jones takes charge of Wolves for the first time in their FA Cup win at Nottingham Forest. **2002** Wolves are embarrassingly beaten to promotion by neighbours Albion and then lose in the play-offs. **2003** Wolves beat Sheffield United in the championship play-off final and finally reach the Premier League.

When FOOTBALL Was FOOTBALL

We ALWAYS win at Wembley

Wolves had been crowned Division Four champions and Steve Bull had plundered an amazing 52 goals in the season by the time the club put the icing on the cake by beating Burnley in the final of the Sherpa Van Trophy at Wembley. Surprisingly, Bull failed to score at the twin towers, but his strike partner Andy Mutch was no slouch either: the one he headed home in a 2-0 victory was his 23rd of 1987–88.

Robbie Dennison, another player recruited from neighbours West Brom, brilliantly curled home Wolves' second goal at Wembley, much to the delight of substitute Jackie Gallagher (left), defender Floyd Streete and a few fans! The gold-and-black following of more than 50,000 is believed to be the largest one-club exodus of all time to a game in England. Not bad for a match between two Division Four teams.

Bully the backstreet international

LEFT: Four goals in 13 England appearances, of which only two were full 90-minute outings, added up to a good return for a striker who never played for Wolves in the top division. And this header against Belgium in Bologna wasn't far away from being a fifth. By netting on his debut against Scotland, Bull became the first Wolves player to score in a full international since Ron Flowers in 1962.

BELOW: Steve Bull made his England debut as a Division Three player – and scored, of course – then went to Italia 90 the following summer early in his and Wolves' long stay in Division Two. With him here on the training ground in Sardinia are Paul Gascoigne and Bryan Robson.

Steve Bull

Where do you start to tell the remarkable story of this down-to-earth Black Country boy? By stressing that Wolves "nicked" him off their fiercest rivals, of course!

Molineux was in an advanced state of decay with a reputation as a virtual mausoleum when, amid the gloom of Division Four football, new manager Graham Turner persuaded his board to back him to the tune of what eventually added up to £64,000 for the West Bromwich Albion reserve striker.

Steve Bull clicked almost immediately in his new surroundings and proceeded to rewrite the Molineux record books. Having fired the club close to an unlikely promotion first time round, his 52 goals in 1987–88 left no room for doubt 12 months later and it was something of a surprise that he failed to score at Wembley in Wolves' Sherpa Van Trophy final success over Burnley.

However, the encore wasn't too shabby. Bull, all raw power and insatiable appetite, rattled in another 50 in 1988–89 as the Division Three crown was added to the trophy cabinet. There were also some England goals, as he stepped out of the lower divisions to play first for the under-21s and then the country's B team. A full cap followed and the skinhead striker they dubbed "the Backstreet International" marked the occasion with a goal on his debut against Scotland.

It was a remarkable rise for a man who had worked in a bed factory while cutting his teeth with Tipton Town. And it was to lead all the way to the World Cup finals in Italy in 1990 after a stunning four-goal display at Newcastle showed he could score in Division Two, too. Sadly, Bull's club career didn't progress any higher than that.

He started to suffer from injuries and Wolves stagnated with the top flight in sight. Not that the goals stopped. In 1992, Bull overtook John Richards as the club's all-time leading marksman and would add over a hundred more before he was done. He finished with 18 Wolves hat-tricks and, by shunning approaches from Aston Villa and Coventry, underlined his fabulous loyalty to the gold-and-black cause.

A highly familiar sight two decades or so ago... Steve Bull celebrates in front of the South Bank before being congratulated by Andy Mutch on another of his 306 Wolves goals. This one was in the FA Cup at home to Sheffield Wednesday in January 1990, and came on the day Bull had missed the only penalty he ever took for the club in a competitive game.

The calm before the storm... Neil Emblen remains in the distant slipstream of Mark Bright in Wolves' FA Cup fourth-round tie at Sheffield Wednesday in January 1995. The goalless draw was marked by Paul Jones's late penalty save from Chris Bart-Williams but it was in the replay that all hell let loose. Graham Taylor's Wolves trailed 3-0 in the penalty shoot-out that followed a 1-1 draw, but sensationally hit back to go through and ultimately reach the quarter-final.

Mixu Paatelainen is bloodied during Wolves' worthy 1-1 FA Cup fifth-round draw away to Premier League Wimbledon on Valentine's Day 1998. Against the 1988 cup winners, the Finn, whose condition receives a check here from skipper Keith Curle, scored his fifth goal of the season – all of them in the cups. The game was possibly unique in that Wolves'

Still packing a cup punch

Alex Rae's late winner in the 2002–03 play-off semi-final away to Alan Pardew's Reading provided one of the noughties' more memorable goal celebrations. The Scot performed his version of a Scottish jig for the travelling fans and, in an era of underachievement at the club, proved to be a fine acquisition. The combative midfielder scored 21 goals in his 119 games for the club but had to be content with a place on the bench for the play-off final.

Achieving the Holy Grail

LEFT: It says something for the refusal of Neil Warnock's Sheffield United side to roll over that Matt Murray was still named man of the match in the play-off final. The giant Wolves keeper highlighted his heroics with a second-half penalty save from Michael Brown.

BELOW: Nathan Blake flicks home the second goal against the Blades at the Millennium Stadium. Three first-half goals had Wolves fans in dreamland following all the promotion near misses, with Mark Kennedy and Kenny Miller scoring the other two.

ABOVE: Promotion winners again... Wolves get ready to party after beating Doncaster in May 2009.

The author wishes to acknowledge not only the fabulous Mirror photographers (who sometimes sit out in the rain while the writers have the best seats in the house) but the other team members behind this book – among them David Scripps, who first offered me this dream gig and then left me like a kid in a sweet shop by granting me access to Mirrorpix's magnificent archive, Vito Inglese, Mel Knight, Elizabeth Stone, Richard Havers, Kevin Gardner and Rebecca Ellis.

Haynes Publishing are responsible for a stirring WFWF series, to which I hope we've done justice.